Grateful
Leadership

Grateful Leadership

Using the
Power of Acknowledgment
to Engage All Your People and
Achieve Superior Results

JUDITH W. UMLAS

Senior Vice President, International Institute for Learning, Inc.

International Institute for Learning, Inc.
www.iil.com INTELLIGENCE, INTEGRITY AND INNOVATION

Bradford WG Public Library
425 Holland St. W.
Bradford, ON L3Z 0J2

New York   Chicago   San Francisco   Lisbon   London   Madrid   Mexico City
Milan   New Delhi   San Juan   Seoul   Singapore   Sydney   Toronto

The **McGraw·Hill** Companies

1 2 3 4 5 6 7 8 9 10 DOC/DOC 1 8 7 6 5 4 3 2

ISBN 978-0-07-179952-2
MHID 0-07-179952-4

e-ISBN 978-0-07-179953-9
e-MHID 0-07-179953-2

Library of Congress Cataloging-in-Publication Data
Umlas, Judith.
   Grateful leadership : using the power of acknowledgment to engage all your people and achieve superior results / by Judith Umlas—1st Edition.
      pages cm
   Includes bibliographical references.
   ISBN 978-0-07-179952-2 (alk. paper)—ISBN 0-07-179952-4 (alk. paper) 1. Leadership. 2. Employee motivation. I. Title.
   HD57.7U526 2012
   658.4'092—dc23

2012032461

McGraw-Hill books are available at special quantity discounts to use as premiums and sales promotions or for use in corporate training programs. To contact a representative, please e-mail us at bulksales@mcgraw-hill.com.

This book is printed on acid-free paper.

I dedicate this book to all of you trailblazers who are either being or becoming Grateful Leaders. You have chosen to put yourself on an extraordinary path, and I applaud you for your courage, your commitment, and your humanity. May this book make a true and ongoing difference in the practice of your Grateful Leadership, and may you become an inspiration to others who are considering this path.

In gratitude and appreciation,

Judith W. Umlas

Contents

Foreword

When Judith W. Umlas asked me to write a foreword for her book describing the benefits and joys of being a Grateful Leader, I was honored to do so. I have personally learned that the nation's workplaces are not rigid fortresses. They are living entities in flux, and their growth is dependent on the shifting currents of humanity in and around them.

A culture of Grateful Leadership starts with leaders who are inspired by a profound sense of personal gratitude. They are also acutely conscious of how an attitude of appreciation affects both employees and the community at large. If the expression of gratitude is contrived, the result is uninspired. We all know when someone is being disingenuous, and there is nothing more demoralizing than a disingenuous "Good job!"

Without the authentic expression of gratitude, people can become frustrated and lose sight of the larger purpose. Ungrateful leadership sends companies spiraling downward toward shortsightedness and selfishness. In today's global corporate landscape, loss of purpose ultimately translates into loss of revenue.

In contrast, genuine Grateful Leaders create a culture of appreciation. They move the focus from a "story of me" to a "story of us." They generate a frame for employees, customers, suppliers, and community members who are inspired by purpose and are fully invested in their roles to realize a shared end goal. They are grateful to be part of something larger than themselves. They are grateful to one another. And they are proud to have earned the gratitude that others have expressed to them.

This culture of gratitude is drawing corporations out of the vortex of selfishness and into the interconnected web of humanity. How can a company be only self-centered and express genuine gratitude to stakeholders at the same time? It's impossible. The magic occurs when strength of purpose is coupled with a culture of trust, care, and gratitude. This focuses on optimizing the value for all the stakeholders, which translates to an increase in revenue.

When you create a true culture of care, of gratitude, unbelievable things occur. We would regularly receive amazing letters or calls from customers about their positive experience at Trader Joe's. I would always be filled with gratitude to work with such an inspired team. As an example of the magic that can occur when a team feels fully empowered and grateful, let me share one particular story that continues to amaze me. On the eve of a blizzard, a mother and her small children hurried through our Scarsdale, New York, store to pick up groceries for the family before the storm arrived. She navigated up and down the aisles, worried about the coming storm. Finally, she raced with her family to the cash register with a full shopping cart, her groceries were bagged, and then . . . she remembered that her wallet was still sitting on the kitchen table.

When the mother panicked, the cashier calmly said, "Don't worry. I'll pay for them today. You can just pay me back next time." The cashier swiped his debit card and paid for over $160 worth of groceries. He didn't embarrass her, and he didn't feel the need to call for a manager. He simply acted out of the deep gratitude of service. Here was that culture of trust and care at work in the community. An empathetic culture breeds kindness and gratitude. In that moment and so many others, I have felt inextricably linked to my colleagues and my community through a swelling of gratitude (I'm also grateful that the forgetful shopper returned to the store, paid her bill, and then called me to tell me how grateful she was for the trust she had received).

Judith W. Umlas has written a book about Grateful Leadership at a time when it is vital to have holistic leadership. Her careful thought about this subject (including naming it "Grateful Leadership") is a testament to just how passionate she is about the content of this book. The best writing is born of passion and experience, and Judith brings a surplus of both to the table. Just as gratitude must be sincere, the discussion about its genuine impact in business must be done with heartfelt vigor. Judith is ideally positioned to tackle this subject. She has trained tens of thousands of employees to learn the power of acknowledgment, and she has been exposed to a wide array of individual leadership styles.

Gratitude is an elevating force that links corporations to humanity, thus strengthening relationships that are instrumental to corporate success. There is no question that the spread of Grateful Leadership will improve business by enhancing relationships between people. Who doesn't want to feel acknowledged? Who doesn't work harder when they feel acknowledged and important?

The true measure of a Grateful Leader is when gratitude has become so embedded in the workplace that it no longer needs managerial thrust. When this "orbital velocity" is achieved, companies move along the journey from good to great.

I look forward to the evolution of capitalism into a more holistic and inclusive system of business—one with human narratives of meaning and purpose. And I believe Grateful Leadership will be integral to creating, enhancing, or restoring corporate humanity.

—Doug Rauch, former president of Trader Joe's
and current CEO of Conscious Capitalism, Inc.

Doug Rauch recently retired from Trader Joe's Company, where he spent 31 years, the last 14 as president, helping grow the business from a small, nine-store chain in Southern California to a nationally acclaimed retail success story with more than 325 stores in 26 states. He developed the company's prized buying philosophy, created its unique private-label food program, and wrote and executed the business plan for expanding Trader Joe's nationally. He is currently the CEO of Conscious Capitalism, Inc.; a trustee at Olin College of Engineering; a recent senior fellow in Harvard's Advanced Leadership Initiative; and a member of the board for several for-profit and nonprofit companies. Doug is currently working on a nonprofit solution to the issue of "food waste" and hunger and obesity by bringing high-quality, nutritious food at affordable prices to the underserved in our inner cities.

PART 1

ACKNOWLEDGMENT: NEXT TO SURVIVAL, THE GREATEST HUMAN NEED

Chapter 1

From "I'm Mad as Hell!" to Acknowledgment Activist

Years ago I was troubled by the way people spoke to me or acted toward me at my job at CBS Television while I was pregnant. So I wrote an article for *Working Woman* magazine entitled "How NOT to Talk to a Pregnant Businesswoman."[1] Overnight, I became the authority on this subject, appearing on *Good Morning America* and a multitude of radio stations.

I achieved this notoriety simply because no one else was talking about this phenomenon publicly. I had only opened my mouth (or poised my pen) and offered some commonsense, no-brainer (at least to me) "rules" of communication to create a more respectful environment in the workplace.

For example, I wrote in the article:

"As for touching a pregnant (business) woman's belly, be careful." A thoughtful friend explained the instinctive urge to touch as a wish to "warm your hands at the fire of humanity." A noble thought, but if you have never had physical contact with her before, such an unexpected pat may be offensive. The simple solution is to ask. I was charmed and moved when someone would ask to touch my belly, and I invariably answered yes.[2]

Simple advice, but my colleagues didn't seem to know about it until they saw it in print! And all around me, I discovered people were recognizing the value of what I had written. I found out over time that women were posting the column on their office walls and hanging it up on their refrigerators for years after the article was published!

And so it was that I found a way to channel my frustration over the countless examples of people *not* being acknowledged when they deserved to be. The very first one that I remember taking up residence in the "I'm mad as hell, and I'm not gonna take it anymore!!!"[3] part of my brain was the time I went into my always busy Dunkin' Donuts coffee shop and asked for my usual, mind-bending order of a small, black, half-decaf, half-regular caramel coffee.

This time, there was a new order taker, a lovely young lady with a sweet smile. The next day I returned and got the same person. She filled my order with another pleasant greeting and smile. On the third day, when I got to the front of the very long line, she was there, holding a cup of coffee in her hands.

"What's that?" I asked dumbly. I'm not too bright before my morning coffee.

"Oh, that's your small, black, half-decaf, half-regular caramel coffee!" she said, looking quite pleased with herself.

I was amazed. No, I was incredulous! "How could you possibly remember my order when you have hundreds of customers in a day?" I asked in astonishment. "You are a genius!"

She looked stunned and didn't respond for a few seconds. Then she said very thoughtfully, "I never hear compliments. I only hear complaints. Thank you."

I felt as if I were going to cry when I heard that. How was this possible? How could this delightful, charming, friendly, customer-oriented person be the recipient of only complaints, rather than appreciation, thanks, and . . . acknowledgments? This just was not fair. And so it was born—my need to change this condition that seemed to prevail in the world.

My frustration grew with each incident I witnessed. And now that I was tuned into them, I saw them almost every day. And once again, I felt the extreme urgency to fix this sorry state of affairs. But this time my focus was not one narrow group of people such as pregnant businesswomen. My simple intention now became to change and repair THE WORLD (I tend not to think small)!!!

This intention became fueled continuously by the negative mantra that I now heard over and over whenever I acknowledged someone in a service industry: "Thank you for thanking me; no one ever does that." How awful! How sad! I just had to bring this terrible condition forth and then fix it in a way that would lead to having people who deserved it, be acknowledged in heartfelt and authentic ways continuously.

So instead of an article this time, I became determined to write a book. And so *The Power of Acknowledgment* was born.[4]

The response was phenomenal—both life changing and work altering for all, it seemed, who were exposed to this message. And there were the incredible stories that demonstrated the results to prove this. Along the way, many executives have asked for ways to get their management on board with this soft skill, when their focus more frequently seemed to be on the hard skills.

Ironically, in my opinion the soft skills are the hardest both to teach and to learn. Since it was clear to me that the ability to deliver true, heartfelt, profound, and generous acknowledgments is a critical leadership competency, without which you might as well just forget about leading, it seemed that it was time to write a second book.

From travels all over the world delivering keynote addresses and training sessions on leadership and the power of acknowledgment, I now know, and I have the evidence to support it, that acknowledgment is a skill we all have (although it is in need of development, like muscles that improve when you exercise) and it is one we all want to demonstrate. I've also witnessed the power of acknowledgment—how it changes the lives, moods, and self-perception of both the giver and the recipient, virtually each and every time it is practiced.

I've seen how acknowledgment changes the level of employee engagement, and I've heard about how it affects the bottom line, with the capability of turning average organizations into world-class companies. And I know that leaders who are bold enough, daring enough, self-confident enough to be, of all things, *grateful* to those they lead will have a profoundly positive impact on their teams, on their divisions, on their organizations, and on what they can achieve. And miraculously, this capability is available to all of us, all of the time. So for those leaders who want to practice the truest and the most gratifying kind of leadership available—Grateful Leadership—and who want to reap the rewards, let's get busy! But first, you may ask, "What *is* Grateful Leadership?"

Let's spend a few moments on this.

Chapter 2

What *Is* Grateful Leadership?

In the 1960s a new concept in leadership, known as "servant leadership," emerged with the writings and teachings of Robert Greenleaf. The emphasis in this form of leading was on the needs of the people who were being led, which seemed to run counter to the basic ideas underpinning the more hierarchical leadership philosophies popular at the time. Greenleaf created the concept in 1964 and started using the term then. He wrote:

> It begins with the natural feeling that one wants to serve, to serve first. Then conscious choice brings one to aspire to lead. That person is sharply different from one who is leader first, perhaps because of the need to assuage an unusual power drive or to acquire

material possessions. . . . The leader-first and the servant-first are two extreme types.[1]

Kent Keith, CEO of the Greenleaf Center for Servant Leadership, says of this leadership philosophy, which the center promotes: "If you really listen to your colleagues and figure out how to get them what they need, they will perform at a higher level, which improves the customer experience, which affects business results."[2] It is clear that this type of leadership is effective because it frees people and provides them the resources that they need. People who feel supported produce more effectively.

According to the *Success Magazine* article "How to Become a Servant Leader," many Fortune 500 companies, such as TD Industries, Aflac, and Southwest Airlines, have adopted this approach, and there is evidence that these companies are on the right track. Southwest Airlines' former CEO Herb Kelleher felt that flight attendants were the airline's most important leaders because they had the greatest influence on the customers' actual experience of flying. In the *Success Magazine* article, it states that "those who have flown the airline know that Southwest flight attendants are some of the happiest people in the air."[3] The positive culture that Kelleher worked hard to shape is a highly successful example of servant leadership.

In the American National Business Hall of Fame report on Southwest Airlines, it states that "Kelleher gave his employees the instruction and leeway to 'do the right thing.'"[4] For example, it says, Southwest gate agents were empowered to make decisions and even break rules in order to best serve customers. It goes on to say that Kelleher, in his written communications, often reaffirmed his love for the employees, crediting them with making Southwest a success. It sure seems that something was working and certainly continues to work with that philosophy!

So I am deeply excited to write what follows: I believe that we are on the verge of creating the next wave of vision, inspiration, workability, and success in leadership, which will turn many current ideas and philosophies of leadership upside down: Grateful Leadership.

Aren't employees and suppliers supposed to be grateful to you, the leader, for employing or engaging them, providing for their families, and much more? What I am calling "Grateful Leadership" turns that attitude on its head, and I fervently hope that this form of leadership will sweep businesses, associations, and communities all across the world with an unprecedented rapidity, power, and force. I believe that Grateful Leaders can make huge changes in the very way people do their work and how they feel about what they are doing.

By my definition, Grateful Leaders are those who see, recognize, and express appreciation and gratitude for their employees' and other stakeholders' contributions and for their passionate engagement, on an ongoing basis. Once these leaders allow themselves to feel and express their gratitude, they typically take action to acknowledge, support, and engage their people profoundly, and positive outcomes are then achieved. These leaders really want to know their employees and other stakeholders as people. (See Appendix A.)

Research done by McKinsey & Company identifies personal leadership interaction as being critical to motivating employees. The respondents to a *McKinsey Quarterly* survey asking about what motivates people identified three noncash motivators:

Praise from immediate managers, leadership attention (for example, one-on-one conversations), and a chance to lead projects or task forces—[were] no less or even more effective motivators than the three highest-rated financial incentives: cash bonuses, increased base pay, and stock or stock options. . . .[5]

Walter Robb, the co-CEO of Whole Foods Market, told me the story of a customer who wanted her blind son to have the experience of shopping in a Whole Foods Market. The team member who got the request felt the desire to make this happen, and she got total support from the team leader to create food signs in Braille in three departments. Then the young man was taken from place to place, and it was clear that he thoroughly enjoyed the experience. That is a living example of what I am proposing. The team member trusted that the company's gratitude toward its customers went deep, and she knew she would have the support to step outside the box. Empowering people in this way allows them to make important decisions, encourages them to take initiative, and keeps them aligned with the leader's goals for the kind of customer experience the leader wants to provide. This trust can help to create a culture in which people will take these kinds of initiatives.

Robb also recounted his Grateful Leadership journey:

The real core and secret of Whole Foods is belief in people. When I do store walk-throughs, I don't just "walk through." I spend two to three hours there and ask myself, "Do I feel the spirit? Are team members happy?" I hear people's stories and create space for them to feel acknowledged. And it only works if you are genuinely interested in them. It's also something I kind of grew into. I don't know that I would have walked through stores this way 10 years ago. I was always intuitive but not extremely conscious when it came to dealing with others.[6] (See the complete profile of Walter Robb in Chapter 12.)

Grateful Leaders give their employees and other stakeholders access to them, as well as to other leaders. The book *Firms of Endearment: How World-Class Companies PROFIT from Passion and Purpose* states:

When Honda has a big problem, it implements *waigawa*—temporary suspension of social protocols based on rank—making it possible for workers on the lowest rungs to personally present a proposed solution to the highest executives involved. Harley-Davidson has a similar policy, except less ceremonial: Any employee on any day has access to the highest officers in the company.[7]

By creating a culture of appreciation throughout their organization, in which people truly feel valued, these leaders motivate their followers to *strive for continuous improvement and always greater results*. This, in turn, promotes a positive environment and the overall well-being of both the leaders and their followers. In such cultures, employees and other stakeholders feel valued and appreciated, and they want to stay. Talk about customer loyalty! Retention of your best people—those you invest in, train, and give knowledge to—is not an unreachable goal. It is a natural outgrowth and outcome of Grateful Leadership. Your best people—from employees to customers and even to the suppliers that want to give you their best products and services as a result of the way you show your gratitude toward them—simply won't want to leave this exciting, nurturing environment in which they can thrive. Honda, again, is cited in *Firms of Endearment* in this context: "Honda is said to 'marry suppliers for life'; when a supplier has gained admittance to the Honda family of suppliers, the company does everything it can to help the supplier improve quality and become more profitable."[8] That is a powerful way of showing corporate gratitude!

Whew! That's a lot to ask, you may be saying. Many highly motivated and well-intentioned leaders, who care about their people and how their people feel at and about their work, still have a thought buried deep within their corporate psyches that the people who work for them should be grateful to them and to their companies for giving them their livelihood. Of course, we as workers should not take our jobs for granted, and we should allow ourselves to feel a sense of gratitude for the opportunity to make a contribution to our companies.

But as leaders, you have an opportunity—one that I believe is unique to our times. First and foremost, it is to be deeply grateful for the opportunity you have to lead people in all of the areas we have been discussing. You find yourself in a leadership position. You have most likely worked extremely hard to get to this point. You have faced many challenges and you have made sacrifices along the way, and you want to achieve the best results possible. You want to establish an atmosphere in which the people you lead can thrive, and not just survive. This leadership role is both an honor and a privilege. Not to take this for granted is a challenge, but you must tell yourself every day that this is an "awe-some" task. That is, it is a task of which you can and should and continually remain in awe. Acknowledging your people is a sure way of building genuine trust and a culture of appreciation that can help people give their best efforts.

Walter Robb of Whole Foods says it eloquently:

> I've had a pretty incredible journey. Each experience, good and bad, has helped me grow as a leader. Over time, I've deepened my levels of gratitude for the wonder and intelligence of each and every human being. Having three kids—and raising them as a single father—really gave my life a whole new dimension of gratitude. And I'm still coming into a deeper appreciation of others.[9]

The responsibility you bear for others' lives and their associated challenges is huge, and it should be a source of great pride to you. And then there are your people themselves. They come to work every day, at least in theory, to support the goals and missions of your organization to which you as well subscribe. Each one of them has a whole life—with husbands, wives, children, elderly parents, homes in need of repair, graduations, weddings, baby births and grandchild arrivals, medical issues and bills, and on and on. They all have a commitment to be at their job every day, and how they "show up" depends to a great extent on you!

Of course, outstanding leaders motivate others by developing broad goals and missions that others support and endorse, and by which they are inspired. But in addition to that, how you value, appreciate, and express gratitude for their contributions on a daily basis will set the tone of their work experience. Think of the impact that this kind of positive culture has had on the success of companies such as Southwest Airlines. If you both feel and display a sense of gratitude for what employees bring forth, they too will feel it and treasure it. That you don't take their long commutes, extended work hours during challenging projects, or wonderful contributions for granted will make a world of difference to them and to what they bring forth on the job. Your continuous experience and demonstration of your gratitude brings forth their gifts—more and more of them over time.

Gratitude is one of the deepest forms of affirmative self-expression. Many studies, such as those described in the *Harvard Mental Health Letter* of 2011 "In Praise of Gratitude," have been conducted on the links between gratitude and health, a positive outlook in life, decrease in depression, and much more.[10] Those who cultivate and allow themselves to feel gratitude on a deep level have a pronounced and increased sense of well-being. Why shouldn't that be you? And why shouldn't your people be the deserving recipients of that overflowing gratitude? There is an almost sacred sense of others that Grateful

Leaders can cultivate when they allow themselves to feel gratitude and to lead others in a grateful way. Gratitude is like a powerful force field—when you experience it, cultivate it, and best of all, let it show to the people that surround you, they are drawn to you and to your mission and your vision. Bringing this heartfelt and authentic way of interacting with the people you lead will bring about miracles!

Acknowledgment of who their people are and who their stakeholders are and the contributions those stakeholders make to the leaders' organization is a key tool for Grateful Leaders. The ability to acknowledge others is a critical skill that is not often considered in the usual list of outstanding leader characteristics such as business acumen, technical expertise, communication abilities, and vision. However, skill in authentically acknowledging others may prove to be the true differentiator among leaders—that is, between those who do not inspire their employees and those who do. The choice of which kind of leader you are is yours to make.

So stay tuned. The results will be unpredictably positive!

Chapter 3

BRINGING ACKNOWLEDGMENT— AND ITS BENEFITS— TO YOUR WORKPLACE

*"Next to physical survival, the greatest need of a human being is . . .
to be affirmed, to be validated, to be appreciated."*
—STEPHEN R. COVEY, *7 HABITS OF HIGHLY EFFECTIVE PEOPLE*[1]

For many years, Stella had worked for a hotel company, where she had advanced to revenue manager, a leadership position that put her in charge of three reservation agents. Her performance, as well as that of her agents, was excellent—and she made sure she always informed them of how much she appreciated their fine work. Every few months, she took them out for lunch to show her appreciation, and if one of the agents ever received an e-mail of thanks, she sent it to her director and hung it on the company bulletin board.

Her job was her life: she was a loyal employee, the kind of person who brought in an angel food cake for a birthday, remembered a coworker's anniversary, and showed up at the hospital when someone fell ill.

But over the years, something soured in Stella. Despite her years of service, her excellent performance and loyalty, she was missing an essential element in her work life—one that was so important, so vital, that it drove her to leave her job when she was unexpectedly offered another senior position in a competing hotel organization.

It was something entirely free and easy to convey, yet not used enough in her corporate culture—*acknowledgment*. If you want to engage, motivate, inspire, and keep your best employees—while having them achieve superior results—let them know through your sincere acknowledgments that their worth and importance to the organization are inestimable. Show your gratitude for their efforts and enthusiasm. You will see that this makes the difference between having workers who are unengaged, uncommitted, and lacking passion for what they do and those who are motivated, passionate, high performers.

In all her years, no one had ever told Stella she was doing a great job, or even a good job. No one had taken a moment to acknowledge how important she was to the organization.

Her boss was flabbergasted when she told him she was leaving and why. Could such an ineffable thing as acknowledgment really be this essential to a worker?

Yes! According to a Gallup survey, praise (and therefore, I would suggest, acknowledgment) creates employee engagement. And when workers aren't adequately recognized, they're three times more likely to quit in the next year. This translates directly into dollars.[2] A Gallup study estimates that annual productivity losses in the United States resulting from disengaged workers is a whopping $300 billion! This projection is based on more than 30 years of Gallup's in-depth behavioral economic research involving more than 17 million employees.[3] The evidence for the bottom-line impact is astounding!

In Stella's case, after she left for her new job, the HR manager sent her a list of praiseworthy comments from fellow managers and heads of departments that they had documented during a management training exercise that had taken place the week before Stella left. The managers had chronicled how much they admired her work and valued her contributions. Had Stella received this list earlier, she probably would not have left at all. But by then it was too late.

The Stella story was, in my estimation, a corporate tragedy, one that occurs on a regular basis. Think about how easily it could have been avoided. And think of the costs involved in training her successor and more. A Society for Human Resource Management (SHRM) study on retaining talent tells the sad and dramatic story this way:

> Employee departures cost a company time, money, and other resources. Research suggests that direct replacement costs can reach as high as 50 to 60 percent of an employee's annual salary, with total costs associated with turnover ranging from 90 to 200 percent of annual salary. Examples include turnover costs of $102,000 for a journeyman machinist, $133,000 for an HR manager at an automotive manufacturer, and $150,000 for an accounting professional.[4]

But now I'm going to share with you another real-life drama, and happily, this time it is an amazing and positive one. It's one that demonstrates the true power of acknowledgment, against all odds, in a team leadership context. And it is told in the words of the leader who experienced this power firsthand:

I'm always excited at a project kickoff—the hopefulness and the initial enthusiasm about the project always puts me in a good mood. But on this day, my kickoff happiness was tempered when I realized a certain person was assigned to my team: Jim was my technical lead, and I was grouchy about it. I walked away from the kickoff mumbling to myself about how I would have to put up with this guy's negative comments—he never had a positive thing to say about anything. At every meeting, he would interject with statements like "No, that won't work," or "You will never complete that on time," and to be honest, he just irritated me. I decided to sit down and have a good talk with myself—this guy was on my team, and no amount of whining or wrangling was going to get me a new technical lead, so I had to just deal with it.

About that time, I remembered some of the concepts I had read in Judy's [first] book: I remembered that acknowledging someone could change his or her attitude, and I thought that doing something different might change the dynamics of the situation. In our next team meeting, Jim did his usual—he shot down every idea and ridiculed every deadline we set—and as usual everyone ignored him and kept talking about our project.

But this time, I stopped and took a breath, and I said, "Jim, can you tell us more about why you don't think we can do this?" He looked shocked. The whole team stopped talking and turned to him.

I said, "Go ahead, Jim, we're interested . . ." He was taken aback. He reddened in the face a bit, but he actually put his thoughts together and made a very logical argument about a point we had missed. I said, "Wow, I'm glad you pointed that out, Jim. I totally missed it. Could I ask you to take that one step further and help us understand what we should do to resolve the issue?"

He said he would have to think about it, which, by the way, was fine with me because he didn't speak for the rest of the meeting!

Later, I stopped by his desk to discuss the issue more; I needed a risk-mitigation plan for the issue he had uncovered. I started the conversation by thanking him for discovering this issue—after all, had we not addressed it, the project could have been in trouble. He was so disoriented by now, he didn't know how to respond, but I expected that—Judy reminds us in her book that some people cannot accept the acknowledgment we give—so I wasn't put off by his confusion. Some time later, he came up with some ideas about handling the issue, and we actually experimented with some of the solutions to understand what might work. He did excellent work, but no one ever knew it because of his negative attitude.

Over the course of the project, I kept quizzing him about possible problems and solutions and praised him privately for being my "failure analyst." I pointed out to him that it is a great and essential skill to see the weaknesses in a plan. I have a tendency to leap first and look later, so his skepticism kept me out of trouble more than once. After that, he took an active role in project meetings, even to the point of leading some meetings to analyze issues. At the end of the project, I made a special trip over to his desk to say thanks again for his overall efforts, and he told me something so interesting. He said, "You are the only person who listened to me. Everyone always ignored me, but now I know I have something important to say." That statement knocked my socks off. . . . I'm not a great people person, but I think in this case, a simple acknowledgment formed a good and productive relationship with someone who provided a key need to the team! Thanks, Judy!!![5]

So now you have a sense of how you can use the power of acknowledgment in your leadership role, and some of the results it can produce—for you, for your people, and for the bottom line. Acknowledging Jim resulted in his total engagement in this and many subsequent projects, and his input saved the company from making huge, costly mistakes. The project leader's appreciation and Grateful Leadership (not taking his contribution for granted, for example) made a huge difference to Jim's productivity and to the success of the project. It's so simple, isn't it? And of course it goes without saying, but I will say it anyway: there needs to be a balance between acknowledging effort and good results, and holding people accountable for their performance.

No matter what you are starting with, you can create a corporate culture of appreciation and acknowledgment—right here, right now! As Stephen R. Covey says, "One person can be a change catalyst, a 'transformer,' in any situation, any organization. Such an individual is yeast that can leaven an entire loaf. It requires vision, initiative, patience, respect, persistence, courage, and faith to be a transforming leader." Using the power of acknowledgment, you can be the "yeast"! Be that transforming leader that Covey describes.[6]

My previous book, *The Power of Acknowledgment*, focused on both personal and professional relationships. And after traveling many thousands of miles and working with tens of thousands of project managers, engineers, executives, managers, vice presidents, and presidents, I now see how hungry leaders and potential leaders are for this simple but powerful message and its application to their places of work.

So here's the cold, hard truth: You simply *cannot* be an effective leader without the ability to deliver profound, generous, heartfelt, and authentic acknowledgments to those who deserve them. Period! And you also need to be a Grateful Leader: when you show gratitude toward your people for their contributions, this will make a huge difference in your workplace. Yes, there are other ways to lead. Steve Jobs was noted for being remarkably difficult and yet producing great results.

In the *Harvard Business Review* article "The Real Leadership Lessons of Steve Jobs" by Walter Isaacson (also author of the book *Steve Jobs*), the author wrote:

> One of the last times I saw him, after I had finished writing most of the book, I asked him again about his tendency to be rough on people. "Look at the results," he replied. "These are all smart people I work with, and any of them could get a top job at another place if they were truly feeling brutalized. But they don't." Then he paused for a few moments and said, almost wistfully, "And we got some amazing things done."[7]

So yes, you can get great things done while *not* practicing Grateful Leadership and by being rough on people, but the path is a lot smoother and your people will be a lot happier when you do practice it. Still, while Jobs may have been hard on his people, they received acknowledgment from the global market knowing that they had a role in producing such "cool" and successful products.

To make it easier and more immediate to create or enhance a culture of appreciation and acknowledgment right here, right now, I have created a framework and a foundation of this work for you that I call the "5 Cs." Understanding the 5 Cs will bring a new consciousness and awareness to you, a consciousness of both the benefits and the obstacles you experience to acknowledging people fully, generously, and profoundly, in ways that directly affect your organization's position in the marketplace and your bottom line. The 5 Cs will set the stage for the 7 Principles of Acknowledgment that follow in Part 2.

Chapter 4

The 5 Cs: The Acknowledgment Practice That Works Miracles

Now that you know you are the yeast that will cause the whole loaf to rise, you need to know how simple it is to make that happen. That's where the 5 Cs come in. So just relax—this will be easy, fun, and momentously fulfilling. It also sets the stage for creating and launching your *Acknowledgment Action Practice*.

Let's first take a minute to define *acknowledgment*. I want to do this now, before we really get going, so that we are all clear on the concept that is my passion and my purpose. Once, I was brought in to speak to a group of mediators and lawyers in Southern California, and my presentation "Leadership and the Power of Acknowledgment" had been accepted, publicized, and promoted for several weeks before the event. When I got to the group of about 30 people, I began to speak about the definition of *acknowledgment* that I am about to give you. "Oh, no!" one vocal participant shouted out. "That is not what we wanted you to speak about. We want you to talk about how acknowledging two different parties' points of view is critical in mediation, as well as in legal situations." I smiled and shrugged, and I offered to leave, as that was not what I was planning to speak about. "Well, go ahead, then," another one said. And by the end of the presentation, the group understood the concept and power of acknowledgment as I define it. Later, I was asked by one of the members to speak at another group of mediators and lawyers a few months afterward. So here's what I mean by *acknowledgment*, and if you don't like it, please return this book and buy another!

Acknowledgment, by my definition, is the heartfelt and authentic communication that lets people know their value to their organization or to their team and the importance of the contribution they make. I have identified the foundation and underpinnings for acknowledgment as the *5 Cs*.

The first C is for *Consciousness*. Most people are simply not aware of the frequent acknowledgments that inhabit their minds—they take note of them in a way similar to watching pretty colored tropical fish swim by in a tank. But that tank is your brain, and if you watch the acknowledgments "swim by," you will not "catch" and then deliver them unless you take the next step. One participant in an e-learning seminar about the power of acknowledgment sent a text message to all of the participants—about a hundred of them—in the middle of the webinar. He wrote, "I'll be right back. I have to go acknowledge my boss!" He got a round of virtual applause, and he "stepped out" for about 10 minutes. When he returned, he texted everyone with these words and punctuation: "I did it!!!"

Why did he acknowledge his boss right then? Was it that it had just occurred to him for the first time that he really wanted and needed to acknowledge his boss? No, he had undoubtedly told himself hundreds of times how much he admired his leader's management style, his accomplishments, and his communication. But it was the *conversation* about acknowledgment that generated the Consciousness. Reading about the 5 Cs will be exactly what you need to lay the foundation for actionable and grateful acknowledgment. You can start becoming conscious of the overwhelming and overflowing gratitude you feel— yes, it is true, when your people perform with excellence and agility, it's almost as if you are a proud parent! But do you "speak" that gratitude? Usually not, and so it dissipates and dissolves.

So now once you begin to become conscious of the acknowledgments that are floating around in your brain, then the next C is for *Choice*. You can always choose *not* to deliver the acknowledgments to the people you work with—but at a cost. The fact that you appear ungrateful and unable to even thank people has a price tag, and the price is steep. The cost to you and to your organization is what you lose: their engagement, their loyalty, and their desire to please you and to make you proud of their accomplishments. So I always urge you to make your Choice a *yes* whenever possible.

Of course you have to set high standards, and you should make those standards clear and your people accountable. But one does not negate the other. When you spot something worthy of acknowledgment, when you are touched, moved, or inspired by a person's actions or abilities, you can and should make yes your choice. But I can't obligate you to do that. When you do choose yes, you may experience a variety of emotions and obstacles: embarrassment, vulnerability, fear, self-consciousness, discomfort, and many more. We are creative with our reasons that have previously stopped us from delivering these precious "gifts" to our people, even when we feel grateful to them. When you are missing some of the other Cs, you buy into the obstacles everyone experiences to moving forward on this positive path. So here are the rest of the 5 Cs that you will need.

The third C is for *Courage*. You may think I am exaggerating when I say it takes *Courage* to give someone a heartfelt, generous, and grateful acknowledgment. But trust me (and if you don't now, I predict you will by the end of this book): it takes real, gut-gripping nerve and confidence to tell people how much they mean to you and to your organization. "What if they ask me for a raise?" you wonder. "What if they think I am trying to manipulate them or trying to get them to do something they don't want to do?" "What if they think I am not being sincere?" "What if they think I am being a 'weakling' for acting so grateful to them?" "It's too 'new-agey!' you tell yourself. It takes deep Courage and conviction to get a true and gushing and grateful acknowledgment across to people in a way that they can really take it in and experience it (okay, so you don't always have to "gush," but being grateful will make a huge difference).

And you will know if they are indeed getting it by what happens when they do. It is as if you are turning a light switch on—they appear to "light up," they stand taller, even seeming to grow a few inches, their eyes open wider, and their features become softer. Those of you who need some inspiration to allow your gratitude to "show" can benefit from Walter Robb's admission that he gets "choked up" even in the midst of public speaking engagements, when he feels a sense of overwhelming gratitude for the opportunity he has to reach so many people with his message and his company's great and healthy food. In fact, before he begins every talk, he "centers" himself by focusing on and feeling his gratitude, and he allows it to rush in and envelop both him and his audiences.

At a conference of 1,200 project managers in Brazil, I had the pleasure of meeting one of my colleagues there who was fairly new to the company. I watched him in fascination and awe as he interacted with our customers and potential customers. He leaned in toward them as he listened to what they were saying, but he did not invade their personal space. It was clear as I watched him that he was not planning his next response to what they were saying, but he was simply listening. He was an "open space" for their communication, and they came alive in their interactions with him. Later, I took him aside and acknowledged him for his incredible listening skills. He looked at me as if he did not know what I was talking about. "I was just hearing what they said," he stated, somewhat confused. I let him know how unusual his gift of true listening was, how deeply affected the people he spoke with appeared to be, and what a talent he had. Suddenly, his face broke out into a huge smile, his eyes widened, and he did appear to grow a few inches taller.

"I never knew this was anything special," he said proudly. "I just like to really listen to what people are telling me. Thank you for letting me know that this is my special gift!"

"You set an example for all of us to model and follow," I said, truly grateful to him for making his contribution.

There are benefits to the giver and receiver of acknowledgment. When people get your grateful acknowledgment, you will definitely experience their getting it, and you will feel a real delight that you have been able to deliver your gift to them. Giving and receiving acknowledgment is a feel-good loop through which you can build a general approach to dealing with others.

The fourth C is more straightforward than the others: *Communication*. Once you have Consciousness and awareness of the opportunity for acknowledgment, have made the Choice to deliver it, and summoned up the huge amount of Courage it takes to express it profoundly and authentically, then it is just a matter of choosing how to get it across to someone. It's kind of like the old saying, "There are different strokes for different folks."

You do have to tailor your acknowledgment to the individual—some people will respond as if it is the highest form of praise if you make a public declaration of their excellence and accomplishments. Others will roll over and faint from embarrassment if you convey it in any way other than a one-on-one conversation or a private e-mail or text message. Discovering the best means of communicating your grateful acknowledgment is up to you.

I don't care if it's via skywriting or Skype—just make sure to get it across to them. Watch them "light up" and fill with pride. Watch them come to work earlier and stay later, and watch them want to give more and more to get the job done. It's not a manipulation (unless it is, and then you will know it). Enhanced performance, better customer service, and increased sales are the natural byproducts of your people feeling valued and appreciated. Your valued customers won't be able to stay away! And you will keep your best people around forever. I know at my company, many of us fall into the 10- to 20-year range, and quite a few of us have chosen to develop with the company and finish out our careers here—even the younger ones!

And that brings us to the fifth C—which is for *Commitment*. Once you see the effects of this magnificent catalyst on your people and the results they produce, you will ask yourself how you ever tolerated a corporate culture without appreciation, acknowledgment, praise, recognition, and validation—and without your expressed gratitude—as the foundation for your organization's true mission, goals, and purpose. You will immediately want to make the change, and that change will generate real and unpredictably positive results in everything from the fewer number of sick days your people take, to the higher amount of dollars they bring in, to the number of years they stay with you in a devoted, engaged, and inspired way.

Here's a powerful statement of Commitment by the co-CEO of Whole Foods Market, John Mackey:

> At Whole Foods we practice appreciations at the end of all of our meetings, including even our board meetings—voluntarily expressing gratitude and thanks to our coworkers for the thoughtful and helpful things they do for us. It would be hard to overestimate how powerful appreciations have been at Whole Foods as a transformational practice for releasing more love throughout the company.
>
> —Co-CEO John Mackey, commencement
> address to Bentley College graduates

I am committed to sharing the power of acknowledgment with you as the Grateful Leaders that you are choosing to be, who want to engage, motivate, and inspire your people. I will share it with any people who will accept it (or give them the tools to enhance their capabilities in this area if they already practice it). That's because I strongly believe that we can change our work environments completely, mightily, and immediately. And I remain committed to changing the world, one person at a time, as we use the power of acknowledgment now through the practice of Grateful Leadership, to turn on the light in ourselves and others, in our workplaces, communities, and families.

We have no idea yet what positive forces for good, for sustainable living, and for sharing the wealth that business entities around the world can bring forth with Grateful Leadership.

Now that you have the underlying foundation for bringing acknowledgment to the people you lead, let's make sure you have the specific principles that will make it (almost) effortless to launch and use the Grateful Leadership Acknowledgment Practice on a regular basis, so you can immediately start seeing the results.

For your own awareness, so that you know where you are starting out in this leadership sphere (and believe me, everyone can improve and be more effective at acknowledging people gratefully and profoundly in ways that make a difference), please take a moment to reflect on your current behavior in regard to leadership and the approach taken in your organization. (See Appendix A for this questionnaire.) You may be interested to note that this questionnaire was adapted from the one I presented to each person who agreed to be the subject of a Grateful Leader Profile that you will find in Chapter 12, although theirs was a bit longer. So you are in very good company!

PART 2

MASTERING THE 7 PRINCIPLES OF ACKNOWLEDGMENT FOR "HIGH-INTEREST" BENEFITS

Chapter 5

WHEN SOMEONE DESERVES ACKNOWLEDGMENT, GIVE GENEROUSLY

Principle #1:
Acknowledgment is deserved by many, but received by few.

It will be easier to acknowledge those you lead if you start by practicing your acknowledgment skills on people in your organization you don't know very well, or even know personally at all. Then you will begin making your organization and all of its stakeholders happier, healthier, more productive.

Each day you encounter workers whose names you don't know, who go above and beyond, performing their work behind the scenes—the woman ladling soup in the cafeteria, the maintenance worker who arrives with his bucket and broom moments after there's a mishap, the elderly woman who cleans the bathrooms. Most of these people are not only unacknowledged but they are barely seen. Start by practicing acknowledgment skills on those in your workplace whom you don't know well or even at all—relative strangers who surpass your expectations. As you practice these skills, you will begin making the workplace a happier, more productive environment. Look carefully and you will find those unsung people who deserve acknowledgment.

I have experienced this kind of reaction so often. When I get helpful telephone operators—the ones who try a bit harder than I would expect to find the number I am searching for—I say, "I really appreciate your trying so hard to help me, even when I don't have the correct spelling of the name or the person's street address!" As I say this, I can actually feel, even through the telephone wire, the operators expanding. Sometimes they are dumbfounded, almost speechless. Other times they sound nearly joyful. A few have even acknowledged me for acknowledging them.

During a presentation of a "Leadership and the Power of Acknowledgment" workshop to about 20 executives at a major global company, we hadn't even made it through this first of the 7 Principles of Acknowledgment when a participant, a senior leader named Tom, started waving his hand rather frantically in the air. I called upon him, seeing that there was some urgency in his desire to communicate. And I could not have written a better script for this class than what he stated:

> Our company is about to celebrate its fiftieth anniversary. And a few days ago, I was looking through one of the anniversary books with pictures from the past. I saw a woman sitting at a reception desk in the company lobby. I did a double take, and I looked more closely. That very same woman is still sitting out in the main lobby right this minute!

Everyone started to mumble and mutter, and they joined him in his forthcoming observation:

> She is and has always been an outstanding representative of the company. We have many global visitors, and she handles each one with professionalism and great caring. She finds us for them when they arrive bleary-eyed from long, tiring trips from Europe. She makes sure they get what they need, and she couldn't be nicer to us and to these visitors. And I don't think I ever truly acknowledged her for her contribution to our company and to our staff! How could I have missed doing this? I think I need to go out there right now and do it!

I told him I thought it was a great idea. He jumped out of his seat and started running for the door.

As he was almost through it, I offered him a copy of *The Power of Acknowledgment* to give to her. As he ran to the front of the classroom to get it, everyone was buzzing about his intention, and many said they wanted to join him but decided not to so they wouldn't overwhelm her.

Several minutes later, he reappeared in the class, and I can only describe his face and his composure as "altered." It was clear that he was totally moved by the interaction he had had with the receptionist, and we all waited anxiously to hear what had transpired. "I told her how much all of us have appreciated her many years of excellent service," he said, appearing very moved. "I gave her the book, and I explained that we were participating in a course on acknowledgment, and I wanted her to know how much we valued her great service. She started to cry," he said, choked up, himself. "And then she told me that after she reads the book, she will give it to her daughter and granddaughter and make sure that they, too, read it."

He and the others in the room, who were planning to go up to her individually when they left the class, found it hard to believe that they had not ever fully, profoundly, and generously acknowledged or verbally appreciated the superb service that she had given to all in her 50 years of working at the company. Yes they had been polite, yes they had thanked her, but no one, they agreed unanimously, had ever let her know her true worth to them and to the entire company.

It was clear that on this day, the dedicated receptionist learned that her entire career had been worthwhile—that it had made a huge difference to countless people at this company and around the world. There is no greater "50 Years of Service Award" that she could have been given than this acknowledgment. And the totally terrifying part of this story with a happy ending is that it might have been only a week or a month, or even a year before she retired or even passed on, never knowing the difference she had made to so many people on an ongoing basis. What a deep personal loss this could have been to this fine example of excellence, dedication, and commitment.

I thanked Tom for jumping out of his seat to fully acknowledge this very deserving person, at the very moment that he realized it was wanted and needed. Bravo to him! He was doing what leaders can and should do, on an ongoing basis. If we are willing to speak committedly and generously and gratefully from our hearts, we can all help others experience the true meaning of their service to an organization. It is your privilege and your challenge as a Grateful Leader to make sure that your people know how valuable their contribution is! The company was fortunate to have someone who could still deliver excellent service over such a long period of time, but many others would not have done this. Without the profound appreciation they felt they deserved, they might have been "out the door" or else performing at a much lower level after a time.[1]

The positive effects of the power of acknowledgment can be seen in unexpected places such as the training academy of the New York Police Department (NYPD). Captain Daniel E. Sosnowik, the commanding officer, Leadership Training Section (LTS) of the NYPD, recounts the following story. What he illustrates here is the benefit to the organization as well as to individuals that occurs when you take the time to tap into and acknowledge others for their strengths, experience, and accumulated wisdom:

> I'm fortunate that my duties also take me out on patrol twice a month, as a "duty captain." I travel throughout one of the patrol boroughs of the city (in my case, Brooklyn South), visiting precincts, reviewing conditions, responding to large-scale emergencies, and conferring with supervisors. As my tenure here at LTS increases, I come into contact with more of our graduates, and I'm gratified as more and more of my students remember me from their time in our programs. I always take a few minutes to "pick their brains," looking for information regarding their own experiences, and I explain that the information they share may serve to help me further update our curriculum back at the academy and address current concerns. As always, they are involved—just as they were during the actual training. Few things make people feel as good as knowing that their opinion is sought and valued.[2] (See the complete profile of Captain Sosnowik in Chapter 12.)

But why focus on relative strangers or people we see from time to time at work but don't know well? Because doing a good job of delivering a whole-*heart*-ed acknowledgment of someone can be harder than it sounds. It makes sense to try it out on people who aren't as close to you as the people you work side by side with. Relative strangers will be pleasantly surprised, and they are not likely to waste time worrying about your motives. And when you make someone's day, you make your own, and everyone benefits.

That's what happened to me in an experience I had not long ago.

I was at a New York airport preparing for a flight when the security agent stopped me and studied my boarding pass. He looked at me, and then he looked back at the pass again.

"You're not the same person on your driver's license as on your boarding pass."

I was very surprised since I didn't make a habit of checking my boarding pass (shame on me).

There had been a mistake. The gist of it was that I had been given the wrong boarding pass, and I had to return to the counter to pick up my correct one. I was already a little late for my flight and understandably nervous.

But the transportation security agent, a man named Richard, was extremely kind and calm with me. He didn't make me feel as if I'd done anything wrong, but instead he told me exactly where to go, and he tried to do everything he could to speed my return trip along.

"Now when you return, come see me," he said. "I'll make sure you get through right away, so you don't have to stand in line."

In this crowd of pushing, anonymous people, I felt so personally looked after and cared for.

The transportation security agent did as he promised: upon my return, he stood beside me like a caring parent and whisked me through the line, giving me a bright smile as I left.

When I got to the other side of the security operation, I realized I had a few minutes to spare before my flight, and I asked for the supervisor of the transportation security agent. I was told he was not on duty at the time, and when I asked to write a note to him praising Richard, the person I spoke with sounded flabbergasted.

"Praise? We don't have a form for that. The only forms we have are for complaints."

"Well, give me that, and I'll change it to fit."

I filled out the form and said that I had felt very well taken care of by this agent and I appreciated the way he had gone over and above what I felt was required to help me. I put my e-mail address in the note, never thinking I would really hear back from him, even though I secretly hoped I would.

Soon after, though, I received a note from the security agent's boss. He said how happy he was to receive the good feedback about his worker—and how rarely this kind of communication took place. In fact, he was going to give the security agent the note and hold him up as a model of how to deal with the public at the next agency meeting of the Transportation Security Administration (TSA) personnel. I was thrilled to hear that.

Not long afterward, I got an e-mail from the agent himself. "In 15 years of working, yours is the first compliment I've ever received," he told me. "I'm walking on air, and I will now go and tell my 90-year-old mother about this!" I was even more thrilled, but I was also saddened by how long this high-performing and well-intentioned agent had had to wait for an acknowledgment from a passenger.

With a simple, caring act of appreciation and acknowledgment, we simply have no idea of the contribution we make to someone who talks to thousands of people without any human(e) interaction. I suspect that Richard's leader knew the difference it would make not only to his agent but also to the many agents he supervised to see an example of one traveler's positive response to an agent's actions. All of the agents could benefit from having Richard be acknowledged—it would give them a model of thoroughness, politeness, and warmth to follow, and they could all use it to improve customer service. Everyone benefited!

Here's another great story about a person who was seen every day by a worker in a corporate office but who was not fully appreciated or acknowledged. At a webinar I led, I heard the amazing story of Willie, the security guard at a major office building who *knew the name of every person in every company in the building*—we were talking about thousands of people!

The woman who shared this story with us was embarrassed and even ashamed that she had never told Willie what a difference it made to her when he greeted her by name and with a smile, every time she entered the building. And though she had heard about his uncanny ability to welcome everyone by name, but she had never communicated how much it meant to her and, she assumed, to thousands of others. "Will you do it? Will you tell him?" I asked her. "Of course!" she said with conviction. I decided that Willie was such an acknowledgment-worthy worker that I autographed a book for the webinar participant to give to him. Knowing the difference he makes to others *has* to make a difference to Willie!

And Willie can also be an inspiration to Grateful Leaders, who have the opportunity to make their people feel *known*! A CEO who walks through the hallways and greets people by name or asks them about their children whose names this Grateful Leader happens to remember will be held in extremely high regard. When it comes time to take on a new challenge or to take initiative, the person who feels known and appreciated will be much quicker to do so than the person who doesn't feel appreciated. Ultimately, employees' feeling acknowledged can and will affect the bottom line, as people show the willingness to take risks or to make personal sacrifices to move an important project forward.

I maintain that much of the world's pain comes from people feeling that they are not good enough, smart enough, or rich enough. They believe they can never get enough of whatever it is they think they need in order to feel good about themselves. These negative feelings are what drive them to do things that make the world seem "broken."

Changing just this one aspect of human behavior on a colossal scale might solve many problems. And—wondrously—it is within our power to start doing this immediately within our own personal universe, which contains the world of work. What if all leaders started acknowledging the people around them for the good things they do, for which they personally are grateful? What if you as Grateful Leaders acknowledged the people around you for the talents they possess and the "gifts" they are to others?

Acknowledgments are contagious—your letting people know that you value them will set the example and lead the way for them to acknowledge those with whom they work. Not all of your workers are great at everything they do, but when you acknowledge them for what they are good at, they will want to do more of those kinds of things and to get better at what they do. Enhanced performance is a natural outgrowth of feeling valued and appreciated. And within the culture of appreciation that you are creating, people will be open and eager to improve what they may not be so good at.

Chapter 6

When Merit Is Recognized, Trust and Loyalty Will Follow

Principle #2:
Acknowledgment builds trust and creates powerful interactions.

Acknowledge the people around you directly and fully, especially those with whom you are in a close working relationship. What is it about your executive assistant, your team leader, your boss, your mentor, your oldest colleague, or your subordinate that you want to acknowledge? Look for ways to say how much you value them, and then be prepared for miracles! Show your profound, heartfelt gratitude and appreciation on a regular basis.

An acknowledgment is a way to cement your bond with a worker or coworker; it's different from a simple thanks. A thank-you is a social custom, an act that's expected. You don't acknowledge a worker for giving you a holiday present; you thank him. But an acknowl-edgment is frequently unexpected, which gives it even more power. Because it's often spontaneous, it is an act that has the potential to make you see someone in a different way—and them, you.

Think about it now:

What are the traits that you could acknowledge about your col-leagues, manager, team members, and employees?

The way they assume responsibility?

How they cooperate and collaborate?

The way one embraces diversity and another keeps the big picture in mind?

Have you told them how you value them for these traits?

If not, why not?

Stephen M. R. Covey has written a lot about the importance of trust in an organization—for example, in his book *The Speed of Trust*.[1] It would seem that one of the positive consequences of acknowledg-ment is that it helps build a feeling of trust. People who feel appreci-ated are not fearful that they will be "burned" if they make a good faith effort, or if, heaven forbid, they make a mistake! The feelings of appreciation motivate employees to reach out in areas in which they may not feel completely secure but in which they can trust that they can and will be supported by their Grateful Leader. What a gift that can be, both to the Grateful Leader and to the employees.

Yet acknowledgments can feel awkward and embarrassing if you are not practiced in this skill. Someone once told me that embarrass-ment was *the* reason she did not acknowledge people at work who definitely deserved it. She said that before taking a class on the sub-ject of acknowledgment, when people did outstanding work and the thought went through her mind that they should be praised for their contribution, even though she "rehearsed" what she would say in advance, she just knew it would be too embarrassing for her to attempt to actually do it. So she just hadn't done it, and she did feel bad about it. But once she recognized that embarrassment was just her excuse for withholding her appreciation, she had the profound realization that she could be embarrassed and still acknowledge her colleagues! She was incredibly excited about this discovery—for her, it was the most valuable insight she could have received, and she couldn't wait to be embarrassed the next time and still let people know how valuable they were to her and to their team. It was a breakthrough!

Quite often, my colleagues at work tell me how great other employees are. When I go and congratulate these employees for their accomplishments, assuming that it is appropriate for me to pass on what I have been told, I am astounded to discover that the employees have no idea that our other colleagues think so highly of them. Why haven't my colleagues acknowledged these people directly, instead of using me as an "acknowledgment bridge"?

Here are a few reasons people give for keeping their appreciation of others to themselves:

1. I don't want to cheapen my acknowledgment by praising too many people too often. It waters it down and makes it worth less.
2. People might not work as hard if they are told how good they are; worrying about whether you value them makes them work harder.
3. A rare compliment is worth much more than a frequent acknowledgment; it is treasured more.
   (But if a boss were to distribute $100 bills to employees when they did something particularly good, would those bills have less value if they

were given out with great frequency? Not if the employees felt they had deserved them. If they felt they were being given the gifts of money with sincerity and appreciation, the value would never decrease. So it is with acknowledgments—their value won't get diminished by frequency if they are truly deserved and delivered in a heartfelt way.)

4. I'm afraid of singling out someone too often and appearing to have a favorite.

   (It may be true that some people are outstanding and deserve more acknowledgment. The Grateful Leader has to help all of their people achieve, to gain the acknowledgment. The role of good and Grateful Leaders is their ability to grow and develop their employees.)

According to a study by the Society for Human Resource Management (SHRM), the number one reason people give for leaving their jobs is that they "do not feel appreciated."[2] As a leader you need to look for ways to say how much you value your employees. If you succeed, you can expect amazing things to happen. Your gratitude, something basically unheard of in the workplace, is a vital gift to them and one that engages them powerfully if the gratitude is followed and expressed by an act of acknowledgment.

Here's a story I was told by a man named Ralph, who made his career in banking and became a senior vice president at a major bank in New York City:

When I got involved in a project that committed me at a level greater than my job would normally have required, I did it because I had a sufficiently developed sense of passion for the results I was likely to generate. The presumption that these results would benefit my company in more ways than could ever have been repaid by financial remuneration meant that I expected that a sense of "job well done" would have been forthcoming. Over a 30-year career in banking, I have been through this type of scenario on numerous occasions, and I have found myself to be greatly disappointed when the anticipated accolades were not forthcoming. While it is my nature to give my best when asked to take on a job responsibility, this disappointment was experienced once too often, and it was truly at the root of my taking an early retirement.

It would have been so easy for the bosses to simply acknowledge the supreme effort put forward toward the greater good of the institution. . . . They didn't. . . . They lost a good employee.[3]

And don't forget about the ripple effects of grateful acknowledgments—those who feel valued and appreciated by our acknowledgment of them want to pay that forward and make others feel that way too.

Sometimes leaders think they are acknowledging people when they are actually recognizing them. Recognition, like a thank-you for a job well done, is valuable and valid. But it is not the same as acknowledgment. And in my estimation, it has a different kind of impact. I had the honor of being the closing keynote speaker at the annual conference of an organization called Recognition Professionals International. While roaming from session to session leading up to my presentation, I almost felt as if I had died and gone to heaven! Most of the attendees were full-time Certified Recognition Professionals® (CRPs), which meant that many of their full-time jobs were to make sure that employees in their respective companies were recognized for their good work and their contributions toward achieving corporate goals. Imagine that!

Simple thanks and the very varied and worthwhile forms of recognition that exist in companies today are extremely valuable. I approve of most, if not all of them: awards, rewards, recognition ceremonies, write-ups in corporate newsletters, and more. However, these are not the same as acknowledgment and they don't take its place. All three overlap and add to the capabilities of Grateful Leaders to make their people feel valued and appreciated. Therefore I call this the Appreciation Paradigm, and this is how I envision it:

The Appreciation Paradigm

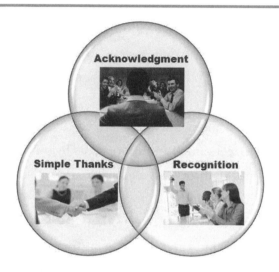

How is recognition really different from acknowledgment? If both are practiced by Grateful Leaders, with equal commitment and enthusiasm, does it make any difference which one leaders use? Yes.

There are two different definitions of these terms that I would like to share with you, followed by the wise words of a business and personal coach that will help drive the distinctions home. You may think I am going a bit overboard by dwelling on these terms to this degree, but I find that it is one of the most profound learnings that people come away with in all of my courses. Many come to the conclusion that as positive as they are with their people, they have never ever *acknowledged* anyone for anything! When I trained 20 military officers, they realized with a kind of dismay that propelled them to action, that although they were decorated (that is, recognized) frequently for their achievements, they were never acknowledged, and they never acknowledged anyone. A good number of them subsequently committed to bringing acknowledgment into the picture as well, one even going so far as to promise to find at least six soldiers he could acknowledge every day! So if it sounds like I am belaboring the point, please let me belabor away—the end result will make it worthwhile.

So first, here are the attributes of recognition:

Recognition

. . . is appreciation for an action by a person

- What they do to help meet a deadline
- The quality of their work
- Their responsiveness
- Their commitment

Next are the attributes of acknowledgment:

Acknowledgment

. . . expresses appreciation of a person for who they are. It may include:

- What you admire and what inspires you about them
- What you see in them that they may not even see in themselves
- Their value to the team and to the organization

And now here are the differences between recognition and acknowledgment as clearly and movingly expressed by personal coach Inez O. Ng:

When you acknowledge someone, you are articulating what it is about this person that you appreciate, admire, like, are inspired by, etc. In recognition, you are showing appreciation for an action. When you acknowledge someone, you are showing appreciation for who they are and how they are behaving. That is the big difference between an acknowledgment and recognition. Many people give recognition well, and very few offer acknowledgment well.

Let me illustrate with an example. Monthly reports are due in five days, and the data is vital in the next phase of planning for your department. John, whose job it is to prepare the reports, is unfortunately selected for jury duty and will be out for at least a couple of weeks. Sally, who is in the department and is somewhat familiar with the reports, steps up and takes on the responsibility of completing them on time. The task required her to stay late every day, and to defer work on some of her own projects. So, at the end of the week, the reports are done, but Sally now has to play catchup for her own responsibilities.

If you were to only *recognize* Sally, what you might say is: "Sally, I really appreciated your stepping in and completing the monthly reports. Because of your efforts, we met our deadline, and the company can complete the planning as scheduled."

If you were to *acknowledge* Sally, what you might say is: "Sally, I really want to acknowledge your commitment to this department and this company when you stepped in and handled the report preparation. I also want to show my appreciation for your selflessness in placing the needs of the company first, and your dedication when you put in all those extra hours. You are a great team player, and I am so grateful to have you on my team.[4]

If you start putting acknowledgment, as well as recognition, into practice as a Grateful Leader, the results will be outstanding, both for you and your recipients. Try it. I know that you—and your stakeholders—will like it! Even more important, your people will be engaged, motivated, and inspired by your doing so. And don't worry, I'm not asking you to forget your high standards—powerful leaders have us reach and stretch beyond what we think we can do, and then we are so pleased with what we have accomplished. Your standards also need to operate within the culture of appreciation that you establish. You set the standards with caring and with support. Also acknowledge your people for their efforts to reach your high standards, as both are needed.

Janis O'Bryan, the chief information officer (CIO) of Hudson Advisors, learned that the most effective ways to encourage her team to bring their best selves to their work were to assist them in their own learning and development and to support them in their efforts to continue to grow on the job:

My gratitude influences my leadership style and strategy as I strive to foster recognition programs within my group, reward teamwork, ensure that training is available to my team, and always maintain a budget for their development and performance bonuses. I have implemented six-month reviews rather than just annual reviews so that there is a focus on goals and my staff's development. I give special rewards inside the group to recognize teamwork and initiative.

These awards are given based on nominations from peers or others in the company. I work to keep my team growing by rotating the leadership of staff meetings each month, which gives team members a chance to develop their public speaking skills and also gives them a chance to be seen as a leader inside our area.

I do extensive research to make sure that my staff members are paid appropriately in the market and are incentivized to achieve their bonus potential. I feel it is also important to take the time to send appreciation e-mails and courtesy copy peers and to celebrate birthdays and anniversaries by mentioning specific contributions of each person. I try to do small things like bringing in food for no reason other than to celebrate the day. I also have one-on-one or small group lunches with team members to give them time to have my undivided attention to share ideas and talk about their lives.[5] (See the complete profile of Janis O'Bryan in Chapter 12.)

In my company, a valued and treasured senior-level employee passed away after a long and grueling battle with cancer. Many of us in the New York office went to a service held in her honor, at which our CEO had been asked to speak. She spoke very movingly about Rebecca, and then she later sent out an e-mail to the entire company—to locations throughout the world. In it she wrote about who Rebecca was in our company and who she was as a person. It was such a beautiful, heartfelt "eulogy" that I felt extremely proud to work for a visionary leader to whom people mattered so deeply and for a company that had both a heart and a soul.

I wrote that in a note to our CEO, expressing my emotions, feeling a bit concerned that it might come across as "brownnosing." Shortly after I sent my e-mail, I got a return e-mail from her saying she was so glad her words had reached me in the way they had. She hadn't heard from anyone else, and she was a little concerned that people might not have perceived her vivid appreciation the way she'd meant it. She seemed very appreciative that I had written her a message in response to her communication.

If I hadn't written her my acknowledgment, it's likely that she would have continued to harbor these uncertain feelings, and she might have always wondered how her eulogy had been received. As a result of my communication, she knew that she had reached at least one person, if not everyone, with her message, and that meant something to her.

All of us have acknowledgments stored in us. As you start paying attention to them, you will be shocked at the many things you could say to the people all around you that would make their day and change their lives. You may not realize it, but you are shortchanging both yourself and them by keeping the acknowledgments locked away in your mind. They are your "gold" to give away, at no cost to you, with minimal effort and energy. In fact, energy comes to you as you deliver these messages and see how people respond to them.

To help you seize these opportunities, try thinking of a time when you were acknowledged deeply and authentically by a leader. How did it make you feel? Try to remember the specifics of these feelings. What were the effects of this communication on your actions that followed?

You can see what the power of acknowledgment can do for you, your team members, your leaders, and for all of humanity. Join the "Grateful Leadership Team" that is restoring people's innate ability to acknowledge others powerfully, profoundly, and generously. The world will change dramatically and profoundly for the better as a result.

Chapter 7

TAKE THE ANTIDOTE FOR ENVY

Principle #3:
Acknowledgment can help diffuse jealousy and envy.

Acknowledge those you are jealous of, for the very attributes you envy. Watch your resentment diminish and the relationship grow stronger as you grow to accept valuable input from the person you were envying. As a Grateful Leader, you can set the example and model this behavior for others!

At the base of all of us is a shared humanity—whether we spend our days in uniforms or suits or sweats.

When you acknowledge people of whom you're envious, resentful, or jealous, these negative emotions diminish, and you experience the humbling awareness that we are all, in essence, the same. This in turn alters your relationship with these people, and it opens you up to accept their value and input.

I believe that many of the problems we and the world face—from personality disputes to crimes to even wars—stem from envy. You might experience that nasty feeling when you see someone who's in wonderful physical shape while you are winded by walking the stairs, or when you contemplate the rookie who has already sailed far past you professionally.

Jealousy speaks to our deepest fears—that we aren't good enough. Ignoring it won't make it go away, but it can poison your relationship with a particular person, or—if you are like me—with many people. But if you know how to use them in concert, acknowledgment and jealousy can be powerful partners for good. Yes, you can actually use acknowledgment—when delivered freely and truthfully—to reduce or even eliminate this disturbing, negative emotion.

How could that be? While envy or jealousy makes us withhold anything that could cause the envied person to seem better or stronger, the act of consciously acknowledging that person for those qualities actually shifts reality. You can feel the jealousy evaporate in the face of your acknowledgment. You feel it in your gut, you hear it in your voice, and you see it in the other person's face.

I was jealous of someone in my company, named Steve, who was amazingly swift, efficient, and organized in everything he did. If he needed to find anything I needed, such as a five-year-old computer file, he'd get it to me almost immediately, while I would be digging around for hours in my files or my Outlook inbox containing 9,000+ e-mails.

Finally one day I just came out and said it over the phone: "Steve, I'm really jealous of you. You are so organized with your electronic communications and can find anything in seconds that would take me hours to find!"

I could practically "hear" the smile in his voice, and "see" him blushing with pleasure. "I've got a method—do you want to know how I do it?"

I hadn't expected that. "You'd teach it to me? Sure, I'd love it."

Steve then proceeded to demonstrate his magical methodology to me for the next hour. I came a long way in that personal tutorial, and while I still can't compete with him, I know I can always turn to him for more coaching and greater success. And I love singing his praises to others and giving him the credit for my improvements. After all, he's the one who generously and patiently taught me.

Telling Steve of my envy cleared the channels and opened communication between us. It also spread good feelings; he received them from me and gave them back to me in return. This is the great ripple effect of acknowledgment and the way it disarms toxic conflict not just in the workplace but everywhere. Imagine the impact of a leader's telling the people he or she leads how much he or she envies those people's skills, gifts, or talents! Unheard of, isn't it? And maybe the Grateful Leader might ask for some coaching or sharing of those people's knowledge, or he or she might make it safe for those people to volunteer to coach the boss, which would be even better! This kind of acknowledgment sets the stage for an openness to learning and making that openness a way of being in an organization.

In another realm, I was deeply touched when I received this living example of Acknowledgment Principle #3 from a religious leader who had read *The Power of Acknowledgment*:

Dear Mrs. Umlas:

I want to thank you for the inscribed copy of your book *The Power of Acknowledgment*. It is an extremely thoughtful—and helpful—work. Only a few minutes ago I got off the phone with an old friend of mine who lives in Boston. Although we entered rabbinical school together, he has authored about a dozen books and is still going strong. About a month ago a beautiful and most flattering review was written about his most recent book. After reading that book some months ago, I wrote him a very complimentary letter, telling him how much I had enjoyed his latest. But now, when I read what his reviewer had to say, I was very impressed and toyed with the idea of calling and congratulating him. Yet I wasn't in any rush to call him. Perhaps there was a touch of envy, in that I myself had written only one book! However, having read what you wrote about handling such a situation, I was determined to pick up the phone and enthusiastically share his accomplishment.

Which I did. Well, not only did he sound surprised and pleased at my call but I too felt very good about having called. He has been a good friend since our seminary days many years ago, and my phoning him as I did must have made him feel as I did, that our relationship was still a good and strong one. All of this thanks to you and the impetus you gave me to overcome my rather envious thoughts.

Again thanks ever so much for the copy of your book and for the practical use to which I have already put it. And with all good wishes.[1]

What courage this spiritual leader displayed, which enabled him to overcome his own very human and understandable response to his friend's success! We can all take courage and inspiration from his example, which brings to life the power of acknowledgment.

One other very demonstrative and dramatic example of this principle occurred in a global on-site training session. When we began an exercise in which participants, all leaders, were asked to create a vision statement for their company that embraced acknowledgment, one participant nearly jumped out of his chair with enthusiasm: "We already have such a statement for our people in our company! Do you want to see it?"

Of course I wanted to grab the opportunity, and I asked him to share copies with everyone. We then spent the next several hours dissecting the corporate statement and trying to meaningfully and powerfully respond to the emerging critical need for it to not only be embraced in theory, but in specific and definitive ways that could be made real throughout the company. All agreed that it was one of the most important training exercises they had ever done.

At the conclusion of the exercise, one participant shared with the group that he had always "hated" the guy who had jumped up earlier in the session to be such a help to their instructor (on this occasion, me), and he felt that the person was acting like his usual goody-two-shoes self once again. He told us that he was jealous and that he had always been jealous of this guy for winning points with trainers and managers alike. But he then deeply and emotionally acknowledged his coworker, both for not worrying about possibly being seen as a brownnoser and for making something very valuable happen that wouldn't have otherwise taken place. Do you remember that third C for Courage? He displayed it remarkably and dramatically by making sure to speak directly to the person, and in front of the whole group!

All of the participants ended up applauding both the acknowledger and the recipient for their actions. It concluded with one very sincere and emotional bear hug between the two guys, and it gave us all a beautifully meaningful example of how overcoming jealousy by acknowledging the person's talents or expertise leads to breakthroughs.

I predict that without a doubt, this exchange transformed things forever between them, and that it made a big difference in the success of their work together.

Having an attitude that is inquisitive rather than judgmental can help us to see other people in a different light and learn more about their perspective. What looked like being a goody-goody at first, later became regarded as a strength that this leader actually admired in his colleague. Transformation of the relationship occurred once he could admit this to himself, rather than remain jealous of his colleague's strength. Appreciation and acknowledgment have this kind of transformative effect. They help Grateful Leaders motivate and encourage the best performance on the part of their people.

Chapter 8

ENERGIZE WITH ACKNOWLEDGMENTS

Principle #4:
Acknowledgment energizes people—
lack of acknowledgment diminishes them.

Recognize and acknowledge good work wherever you find it. It's not true that people only work hard if they worry whether you value them. Quite the opposite! As a Grateful Leader, your gratitude and appreciation motivate and inspire them to go beyond what they perceive as their limits. They will want to give you their best performance and will do whatever that takes.

Imagine this scenario: You've worked three months on a rush project. You've been told that you've been picked because of your organizational skills, but you notice that you're the only one staying late after work. You're not only staying late but working weekends and missing family dinners. No one seems to pay any attention to the extra work you're doing. You sit alone under the fluorescent lighting as the hours slip by. You begin to wonder why this assignment was presented to you as if it were an honor. It seems to be just extra work. You're haggard and sleepless, and the project is the only thing on your mind.

Finally, two days before your due date, you finish. You feel so proud. You've saved the company several hundred thousand dollars.

You take the spiral-bound sheaf of documents into your manager's office and put it on his desk.

But he's on the phone when you walk into the office, and he merely covers the receiver.

"Here are the results of the project I've been working on," you whisper, and he gives you a smile, a thumbs up, and returns to his phone call.

All day you sit at your desk in a state of frozen expectation. Surely something tangible will happen at any moment—you'll be called into his office and given sincere appreciation for the fantastic job you know you did. But as the day goes on, your fantasy is reduced. You'd be happy with a pat on the back or a phone call. But nothing happens. Your boss is preoccupied, you tell yourself, but that doesn't help the way you feel.

This incident makes you feel unappreciated, taken for granted, unimportant, and foolish. In the days that follow, these feelings become even more negative: you realize that you're resentful and unmotivated regarding future work. You've lost respect for your manager, and you browse the newspaper for another job.

If this really were you, what effect would this lack of response have on your feelings of self-worth, your motivation, and your opinion of your job and the difference you make to your company? Imagine how positively you would have felt if the boss had acted in just the opposite way.

Had your manager provided you with a heartfelt acknowledgment for the same job, the results would have been entirely different. You would have felt motivated and energized, and you would have been much more likely to take on extra work again.

Incidents like the one just described can go in more positive ways, in which employees feel appreciated and valued. One of our Grateful Leaders, Xavier Joly of Volvo Powertrain, shared his approach to acknowledgment. This example demonstrates how individuals can be empowered and encouraged to take on difficult challenges with support and appreciation:

> At Volvo's Hagerstown, Maryland, facility, I experience a feeling of real gratitude every single day, and I spread it around by spending as much time as I can with my people. I feel that it is my job to empower them, engage them, and raise their self-confidence, and I do this through acknowledgment. This can mean anything from a smile, to involving them in the decision-making process, to providing coaching and support, or just simply and truly listening to them. Dedicated, active listening is one of the truest forms of acknowledgment because it expresses so much in such a simple act; it is as if you are telling the speaker: "You matter."
>
> I truly value my people's opinions, and I make sure they know that. However, there are times when, in order to help your employees, you need to disagree with them! For example, I launched an initiative—a school in Volvo Powertrain, focused on project management. I told 20 senior project managers that I wanted them to

get their Project Management Professional® (PMP) certification in three months, and I assured them that they would have all the knowledge and support needed to pass the exam, as well as commitment from their top managers. They fought me, saying they needed six months to prepare, but I was adamant in my belief that they could pass the rigorous exam in only three—and 90 percent of them did! I think they felt that "the company believes in me, so now I have to believe in myself." It worked![1] (See the complete profile of Xavier Joly in Chapter 12.)

I see this over and over again in my courses when I do this little exercise, and the results are always very similar:

Scenarios Demonstrating Linkage between Acknowledgment and Engagement

Scenario #1—Lack of acknowledgment by manager
- Feelings
- Results

Scenario #2—Heartfelt acknowledgment by manager
- Feelings
- Results

When I lead this exercise in a webinar or virtual course, we use text chat to communicate. The number of responses and the dramatic quality of the descriptions people use in reaction to the first scenario are clear! Here is a sample:

After Scenario #1

JOAN R: I see it as lack of interest on their part.

CHRISTOPHER S: I feel great frustration.

BRENT P: Perhaps I would not go above and beyond next time for that person.

KEVIN C: I would feel let down. I'd think "Why did I go through the effort?"

TASHA: I'd feel unappreciated.

CYNTHIA L: Seems there is no point in trying to go above and beyond because all I hear are about the bad parts [learned helplessness].

LANCE N: I'm left feeling like, "Why am I busting my hump for this?"

BARBARA D: I'd feel not good enough.

After Scenario #2

CYNTHIA L: I'd walk into hell for the one manager who deeply acknowledged me.

LANCE N: I would be left feeling like doing the job was actually worthwhile.

KEVIN C: I feel like I have to work harder.

YVETTE J: It encourages me to do even more quality work.

LISA T: Inspired!

VALDEMIR A: It's kind of combustive!

KARL S: It inspires loyalty.

LYNNDA P: It's the way life should be!

Yes, isn't that the truth? When we are acknowledged, it's the way life should be! I have called these text chats some of "the best management texts" around, and I have urged participants to print them out and leave them on their managers' desks! What could be more clear than these heartfelt and emotional responses to *not* being acknowledged by their leaders and then *being* acknowledged? It really is that simple. It's almost embarrassing to think about how much money companies spend looking for ways to engage their people, to retain their best ones. And the solution is right there, in their hands, and the cost is little more than their expressing gratitude!

Sometimes bosses are reluctant to use acknowledgment because they haven't experienced it themselves or because they're worried about how it will make them appear to their workers.

An employee at a large telecommunications company told me she made a blunder that involved the public release of private e-mails that cost the company not only money but also prestige. She immediately went to her manager, nearly crying about the situation.

"This is my fault—I should have been on top of what was happening yesterday, but I was distracted by other problems. I'm sincerely sorry and promise it won't happen again."

Her boss accepted the apology coolly and cut the meeting short, leaving the employee feeling that he was secretly furious with her. She went back to work with a sense of diminishment and depression. "It doesn't really matter how well I do," was the feeling she was left with. She barely worked the rest of the week, she felt so discouraged.

But the boss had the opportunity to do much more—to be a Grateful Leader. Instead of leaving her in this terrible condition, he could have acknowledged the courage it took this seasoned worker to admit her big mistake. He could have told her that they would work together to mitigate it. Imagine how that would have made her feel. I would venture to guess she would have felt honored, valued, and appreciated, and she would have put her all into making sure that nothing like this was ever repeated and into delivering top performance in everything she was asked to do.

A Grateful Leader also has to help people achieve in order to gain the acknowledgment the next time around. To me, one of the key roles of good leaders is their ability to grow and develop their employees. In the case just described, it would have made a real difference to this employee if her boss had patiently sat with her to explore what could strengthen her skills and judgment for the future. Otherwise, she will be terrified of making more mistakes of this magnitude, she won't take risks that could be very appropriate for her to take, and she will operate out of fear.

In our company, I have heard my CEO say with conviction, "We celebrate mistakes!" Imagine how that makes our people (including me!) feel—bold, almost fearless about failing, and willing to take risks and achieve results that wouldn't be possible if we felt obligated to operate out of a fear of failure or of making mistakes.

So, returning to the employee who made a large mistake, why didn't her boss communicate in this reassuring way to her?

"I've never received this kind of acknowledgment myself, so I feel uncomfortable with it," he admitted when asked. "Also I'm afraid I'll look like I'm soft or like I'm condoning the behavior," he added. Fear stops a lot of leaders from acknowledging, valuing, and truly supporting their people. If you are Conscious (remember the first C!) of wanting to acknowledge people but are afraid to do so, just (forgive me for oversimplifying) look your fear in the face. What is the worst thing that can happen? People will think you are too "warm and fuzzy"? Oh, my gosh, wouldn't that be awful! Look to some of the Grateful Leaders who are profiled in Chapter 12—in particular, Walter Robb, who gets "choked up" when he is about to deliver a talk to an audience because he is so grateful to them and he is so deeply moved by the people he leads.

A person in one of my courses told me that she thought of acknowledging her reports all of the time, but she worried about their seeing her as "too soft." But the major item she told me she took away from my course was this: it is okay to be considered kindhearted and warm, and to acknowledge someone profoundly and generously anyway! I congratulated her—that was a superb takeaway. Now she won't need to be stopped anymore by her innate softness.

Women leaders in particular may worry about this one. Some feel that as they step into power and struggle with holding people accountable, it could be detrimental to them to look like they are ignoring potentially negative things, to appear soft and easygoing. Well, you never have to "go easy." Hold to your standards, while allowing your softness and humanity to emerge at the same time. Kimberly Supersano, chief marketing officer (CMO) of Prudential Annuities, is a prime example of this. She says:

> I hope I am seen as a Grateful Leader. Grateful Leaders believe in people's potential and the value of each and every person they employ or rely upon, and these leaders help them recognize their full potential. You have to understand people's strengths and interests and appreciate what motivates them. Focus on the positive. I am a strong proponent of giving people opportunities to capitalize on their strengths. Focus on strengths and interests, and find ways to align those two.
>
> Here's an example: A person on a team with a background in training and employee development was moved to our department out of necessity, but she always had a passion for her previous responsibilities, and she was not thriving in her current role. She saw a gap in our department that could leverage her passion. So we created a new role for her, and she was so successful that this role was expanded to four different departments. We were eventually able to formalize this role and have her leverage this passion. She became the head of education and experiential learning. She had been doing project management before.

Kimberly shared with us this information about how employees consistently rate Prudential on annual employee opinion surveys:

- A great place to work
- Likely to recommend Prudential as an employer of choice
- Feel pride in working for the organization
- Would recommend Prudential's products and services to family and friends
- Feel valued as an employee of Prudential

Feeling valued as an employee is certainly a key factor in being engaged and achieving superior results.

One of first things Kimberly did in her new role as CMO was to create working teams. She had heard that people were working in silos, without a lot of cooperation or communication. Employees didn't feel valued. So she held one-hour one-on-ones with every employee—80 of them! These sessions were about getting to know them as individuals—to find out about their families, what they did, where they lived, and what their interests were. Now as she continues in this role, she asks them, "What can I help facilitate, and what would you not want to change?"[2] (See the complete profile of Kimberly Supersano in Chapter 12.)

These sessions take a lot of hours, but without a doubt they are worth it—to Kimberly and to her people. Now could you consider this a "soft" approach? I suppose so, but it has a huge impact, and both male and female leaders use it.

Let's look at the opposite approach to what the devastated young lady who confessed her mistake to her leader experienced—one that is more along the lines of what Kimberly does. Here's what my esteemed and long-time business associate Roberto Daniel of Invensys Controls in Brazil, who is truly a Grateful Leader, regularly does with his employees.

Each month he gives both a box of candy and a copy of *The Power of Acknowledgment* or other motivational book to an employee who has achieved the highest results in product development and cost reduction. He calls it the "candy box acknowledgment award appraisal ceremony," or "Candy Box Award." His employees greatly look forward to this event. It is a simple yet effective way of acknowledging his team members for producing greater results while positively encouraging them to work harder. By acknowledging his team members in a sincere and authentic way each month, they work together in a positive, warm, and welcoming corporate culture. And now the award ceremony has been approved for all of Invensys' South American operations.

Acknowledgment is contagious! Here is Roberto Daniel, in his own words, regarding acknowledgment practices that are effective and motivating for his employees:

One way I've acknowledged my teammates is through a formal initiative called the "Candy Box Awards," which honors them for their contributions and unique talents. I speak about their achievements in front of the whole team, and I present them with a box of candy and an inspiring book (very often Judith's *The Power of Acknowledgment*, Jim Collins's *Good to Great*, or James Hunter's *The Servant*—in Portuguese). The ceremony is documented with photos, which are saved to the company's intranet and sent to the entire management team. I'm happy to say that this initiative was well accepted at Invensys, and it has become an official procedure!

Years ago, I set out to acknowledge one of my quality leads at the time. While he was faced with managing a chaotic supply base,

I saw that he was able to endure many stressful challenges with his forthcoming, empathetic nature. I scheduled a group meeting and announced that we would be acknowledging a certain colleague for his achievements. When I announced this person's name, there was a sudden burst of applause—it was clear that I was not the only one who felt he deserved this recognition. The employee was filled with emotion, completely taken by surprise (and I confess that I too blinked back tears, and I was moved by and deeply appreciative of his positive response).

Like Kimberly, Roberto also sets aside an hour for each of his employees. In his meetings, they speak about anything *but* work. And he truly has a sense of getting to know them as people. He conducts at least one or two of these meetings each month, and over the years since he started them, he has conducted over 300 such sessions. That keeps the Acknowledgment Award, or Candy Box Ceremony, from becoming just a ritual—it remains a highlight of the month for both Roberto Daniel and his people—and for me, when I get a monthly photo of a person receiving a box of candy as well as a copy of my previous book! [3] (See the complete profile of Roberto Daniel in Chapter 12.)

Of course, I post this on my blog, and I am as proud of the individual as Roberto and the employee's mother are! When I asked Roberto how he could be sure that after eight years of this, his people weren't getting a bit tired of the ceremony, he said: "I always start the appraisal sessions by telling one story about what led me to recognize that person, and the announcement then follows. And I know for sure—going by body language and the sense I get—that every employee becomes extremely happy, some of them blinking back tears."

Written acknowledgments can also be very effective, with the added benefit that the employees can read them again and again—very helpful on days when things aren't going so well! They take three or four minutes to write, and they can mean a world of difference to your recipients.

It's well known that former CEO Jack Welch sent countless, hand-written notes to GE people, acknowledging, inspiring, and motivating them. According Diane Brady, in a *BusinessWeek* article, "Welch would prod and praise them, sending out a flurry of handwritten notes, or champagne to spouses, for a task well done."[4]

And I, for one, have saved and treasured the notes of appreciation I have received from customers, team leaders, and, of course, my boss!

I will also never forget the handwritten card I received from our team leader after the completion of a huge project, thanking me for my contribution and for helping to make the project a success. It was one of the first times our company had put together a global event in celebration of International Project Management Day, for thousands of participants around the world. It had taken months for us to prepare for it, and we were all exhausted and thrilled at the end of it. But when I got my card, I remember taking it out of the envelope, feeling a sense of shock and joy at the indentations that the ballpoint pen had made on the heavy paper. I kept rubbing my finger over them after I had read what Archie had written. The good feelings stayed with me a long time after that . . . at least until we had to start up all over again the following year!

And please pay attention to the story that an appreciative colleague of Kimberly's wrote to me about her:

After a large launch last year, Kimberly wrote a three-page, hand-written letter to everyone in the department acknowledging us for all our accomplishments and stating how proud she was of the department. Each letter was individualized with a handwritten postscript note at the end, acknowledging something the recipient did. Letters were put in envelopes and placed on each person's desk to find in the morning.

We are lucky enough to have a wonderful example of the letters she personalized to 80 people.

June 20, 2011

Dear Mark,

It's hard to believe it's already been a full year since I returned to Annuities Marketing. As I look back on my time as your leader, I find myself inspired to share some of my personal thoughts and reflections with you.

First, I want to thank you. Rarely does one have the privilege to take an already-extraordinary team and strive to make it better. The talent in our department is unsurpassed in the industry -- both in the results in your efforts (#1 marketing materials) as well as the manner in which you achieve those results (with passion, with collaboration, with integrity). I am truly grateful to be part of this amazing team, and I get excited every day about what we continue to accomplish together.

Second, I know that change is never easy, and this has certainly been a year of tremendous change. Most of the time I'd like to believe change is for the better. I generally see change as a way to re-evaluate ourselves and consider new possibilities. Some changes bring immediate benefits; others take some time to materialize. Sometimes we get it right, and sometimes we miss the mark. But one thing is for certain – change is a reality of life (especially in an industry as fast-paced and dynamic as ours). I hope you challenge

(continued on next page)

yourself to embrace change and remain open to its potential. More importantly, I hope you challenge yourself to influence it. You are the key to making it work, and without your help our potential is limited. Only through open dialog and open-mindedness can we identify the changes that matter most – and use them to help us accomplish more than we thought possible.

Finally, I want to say how proud I am of what you have achieved this year. In addition to supporting the Annuities business, you've played a leadership role in re-defining Prudential's iconic brand and making it even more meaningful to our internal and external audiences. Together, we have found new ways to work with our business partners to strengthen relationships, foster collaboration, and enhance the impact of our efforts.

We've invested heavily in our people and our culture this year – areas that require continuous attention and priority. While we're certainly not finished, I'm pleased with our progress so far. We've added new talent to our team and facilitated career paths to those who have chosen to move on. We've shared new experiences – from Myers-Briggs and personal development workshops to lunch-and-learns and team-building exercises. Our working teams have helped us build a community where we can laugh, play and learn together in greater harmony. We also extended our flex time to help balance our work responsibilities with the even more

(continued on next page)

In the 2008 Towers Watson global recognition study, it was found that recognition of employee performance by managers significantly increases engagement.[5] Other research on the effects of managerial behavior showed that people feel higher respect and admiration for managers who "consistently provide uplifts for them throughout the *important commitments we make to family, friends, and ourselves. I encourage you to never stop growing and to find new ways to raise the bar for yourself individually and for us as a team. I will support you in every way I can, but the most critical steps reside with you. How will you take advantage of the opportunities?*

It has truly been an extraordinary year together, and I look forward to the exciting, new things we have ahead of us. Thank you for all that you do and for giving so much of yourselves to our team and to our business.

Warm regards,

Kimberly

Mark – it has always been an absolute pleasure working with you. Few people take as much pride in their work as you do. You are always looking for creative ways to do things faster and better – offering us new ways to meet the needs of our clients. Thank you for your commitment to your job and your team. Our success wouldn't be possible without your valued contributions. –K.

day." Employees who hear a word of praise say they are "motivated to work harder and are more likely to go out of their way to help their peers or take action that supports the organization."[6]

With so much evidence in favor of acknowledgment and appreciation, I want to give you, the already or about-to-be Grateful Leader, an opportunity to practice this skill. Let's stop talking about it for a few minutes and *just do it*!

Reach out right now. . . . I'll wait!

Now that you have had some practice, the next time it will be easier! I promise!

Also, now that you have reached out and acknowledged someone, how did it make you feel as a leader, perhaps even as a Grateful Leader? Remember the second C: Choice. You chose to follow, not ignore, the instructions above, and you delivered your Communication of appreciation to some lucky person. You found something real to communicate to that person, something of value about that person that reaches you. Perfect! Keep on doing this, and you will be delighted with the results.

Remember, giving a genuine acknowledgment is as moving and enlivening as receiving one. Giving acknowledgment can feed on itself in a positive way. The more carefully you look, the more ways you will find to acknowledge others.

Chapter 9

VALIDATE WITH ACKNOWLEDGMENTS

Principle #5:
Acknowledgment can make a profound
difference in a person's life and work.

We have no way of predicting the profoundly positive impact acknowledgments can have upon a person, a team, a company, or a community. Only by delivering them gratefully, spontaneously, and in a heartfelt way can you know and truly understand the remarkable difference they can make.

A woman I met at a presentation had worked at Booz Allen Hamilton for years and loved going to work every day. She felt valued and appreciated, and she regularly received positive feedback. Then, out of the blue, she received a job offer from another company.

It was for a higher-level job with increased pay. She couldn't resist this double incentive. With some sadness, she left Booz Allen Hamilton, feeling that it was the right thing for her future career.

After a few months, however, she began to wonder whether she'd made a mistake. Despite the perks, she found it hard to thrive, or even survive, at her new company. Unlike Booz Allen Hamilton, her new firm had no culture of appreciation; the managers never acknowledged her for anything, even when she felt she was going above and beyond. People silently performed in their private cubicles and then went home.

This woman came up to me after one of my speeches and said, "I'm an example of who and what you've been talking about." The week before, she said with a big smile, she had quit her new job.

She proudly proclaimed, "I'm going back to my former company, even if I have to take a lower-level, lower-paying job than I had when I left."

I found this amazing and inspiring. Gratitude was so crucial to this woman that she'd leave a higher-paying, more advanced job to return to a company where people took the time to validate her.

Later I called a partner in the company to see whether she had heard of this happening before, and she laughed and said, "I certainly have! We call them the 'comeback kids'! They don't know what they have until they leave it, and then they desperately want to return. We welcome them!"

This, without a doubt, is the power of acknowledgment to engage and keep our best people. There are no substitutes for this validation and appreciation. I have heard so many times that without it, people are not only sad, lacking passion for their jobs, and uninspired; they are also confused! They think they are doing a great job, the right thing, putting themselves out and going beyond what they think is expected of them, and yet they receive no positive feedback. Does that mean they were mistaken, they wonder? Did they really not do such a good job after all? They desperately crave this positive feedback to confirm their self-evaluations, among other more obvious reasons and needs.

There are whole companies in which acknowledgment is completely unheard of—and not only companies, maybe even some countries. That was the surprising fact I discovered when I went to Finland to deliver a keynote presentation called "Leadership and the Power of Acknowledgment." When I reached the building where I was to make my speech, I was met by the program coordinator, who asked me the topic of my speech. He listened to the explanation with a furrowed brow.

"I thought it was simply on project management," he told me. "I'm afraid acknowledgments don't exist here in Finland," he said.

"What do you mean?"

"Culturally, it's not something we do. We perform our jobs, and that's it. This is what is expected of us."

As I headed for the elevator to settle in my room, I heard several other comments related to the topic of my upcoming keynote presentation: "We think it's excessive to be praised for what we're paid for. Acknowledgments must be American." Now I certainly don't get up on platforms in front of huge audiences around the world just to tell leaders about the value of acknowledging others for doing exactly what they are being paid to do. Going above and beyond is always at the root of my message, but when people do what they are paid to do in an excellent fashion, yes, I do believe they deserve acknowledgment for that too. But this was not the real issue. The people of Finland were not eager to probe their national psyche to discover that they too had the innate need for praise and appreciation.

Someone even suggested to me that giving my speech would be a mistake and perhaps I should just skip it. But the more I thought about it, the more I realized that it was probably these employees, more than others in companies and countries where it was more common to be acknowledged for doing a great job, who needed to hear my talk. So I gathered my courage, and I moved up on the podium and gave my talk anyway, not sure what to expect. Now, I do love a challenge, even when it scares me to death. But I figured that these folks needed something more dramatic than my normal kind of opening, during which I make a quick and clear case for the fact that being acknowledged is an innate human need and that we can't achieve excellence in the workplace without it. Uh uh. Not for this group. They would just fall back on their cultural conception that acknowledgment does not exist, and therefore is not needed, in their country. So I took a deep breath and dove in, realizing that I probably was about to take one of the biggest risks of my speaking career.

"I've been told that acknowledgment does not exist in the Finnish culture!" I began, making it deliberately sound like I didn't know what I was doing on a stage in front of 800 project managers from that country. "I have even been advised by some well-meaning people to take a tour of Helsinki and then go home, instead of delivering this speech to you about leadership and the power of acknowledgment!" I could see by their smiles that they liked this direct approach and they found it slightly endearing. "Is it true," I continued dramatically, "that acknowledgment just doesn't even exist let alone belong here?" I saw about 800 heads nod yes.

I took a deep breath, and I went for my very risky next line, which I had thought of as I walked up on the stage and looked out at their faces. "Is it also true that Finland has one of the highest suicide rates in the world?" Again, about 800 heads nodded, this time more vigorously.

"And do you think," I began my unsettling conclusion with power and force, "there could be some connection between these two facts?" The room started to buzz, and I knew I had them. It was a piece of cake from then on.

It was during that speech that I realized something I'd already suspected: acknowledgment and gratitude are human emotions that know no boundaries or nationalities. It doesn't matter if you've never heard of acknowledgment or if you've never been the beneficiary of it in your life. You respond positively when it's given to you.

In the faces in the audience I saw something happen as I spoke— a dawning, growing certainty, and awareness. By the end of the session, people were not just raising their hands. They were waving them with great intention to be called upon, so that they could acknowledge their managers, who just happened to be in the audience. I received a standing ovation for my speech that day. After I returned home, I led a webinar for close to 100 Finnish project managers, and I discovered that one of the participating companies, Nokia, had actually just initiated a new program called *Peer-to-Peer Recognition.* The purpose of the program was to recognize and express appreciation for the time, work, and knowledge of employees who embodied the values of the Nokia company. The response of the employees to this new program was joyful; they may have never received acknowledgment before, but they were thrilled with the idea and its delivery.

What follows is a copy of the certificate the company's human resources department put together to recognize achievement in one of the company's four core values: achieving together. (I thank Nokia for allowing me to share it with you.)

"I filled in this certificate for eight people, and the response I got from each of them was jaw-dropping," Dean Pattrick, Project Management Professional® (PMP), one of the attendees at my webinar, wrote.

Remember, acknowledgment supposedly doesn't even exist in Pattrick's culture. Yet people were thrilled and delighted with the recognition certificates and the heartfelt comments.

He achieved these results because acknowledgment is a human need, especially at work.

As one manager told me after my keynote: "The timing of your speech could not have come at a better time. Finland, and the rest of the world, I do believe, are ripe for the kind of leadership that uses the power of acknowledgment on a regular basis!"[1]

They were certainly ripe for a change, and I'm glad to have had a hand in it. Several years later, the CEO of my company was in Finland, and several people who had attended my session insisted on relating to her how powerful it was that I had been able to "get them" to deliver acknowledgments to people in that audience. They were still amazed and astounded by it. They didn't know how I had achieved that. As I often respond, it isn't me—it's the self-fulfilling potential of the message. It's the innate need we all have, both to be acknowledged, and yes—to acknowledge others. When we give the gift of acknowledgment and gratitude, we are expressing the highest, the most transcendent, and unequaled form of humanity of which we are capable. When you see people "light up" as a result of the gift you have given them, your own light shines more brightly. You bring that home with you, and it affects your spouse, your children, and even your pets! No kidding!

Our Grateful Leader Michael E. Case, CEO of the Westervelt Company, describes what, in his experience, is the power of acknowledgment to truly lift the performance, loyalty, and productivity of employees:

A Grateful Leader is focused on others. Gratitude implies appreciation, and to fully appreciate others one must be genuinely interested in people. It means having trust in the competence of others along with an honest assessment of one's own strengths and weaknesses. I believe Grateful Leaders have a low sense of entitlement and high sense of personal accountability.

My achievement in business can be directly linked to this understanding of servant leadership, and this is often validated by my colleagues through their positive feedback. As a result, our company has formal programs (financial rewards and public recognition) that highlight associates' contributions in the areas of safety, continuous process improvement, and cross-selling. Additionally, the company's leaders have gone a step further to include servant leadership as one of the key behavioral areas in their annual performance measurement. Informal recognition through private and public praise, as well as personal handwritten notes, also helps promote an environment of acknowledgment and appreciation.[2] (See the complete profile of Michael E. Case in Chapter 12.)

That's why I always say that you never know how your own actions will play out and how they will ripple far beyond your imagination.

People may well believe that too much acknowledgment cheapens its intent and devalues its meaning. But I believe that the way to prevent this outcome is to both acknowledge quality work freely and generously and be (almost) equally forthright about giving constructive criticism. It is the balance and, above all, the truthfulness that gives your acknowledgments power. Effective leaders know how to hold people accountable by setting clear and ambitious goals that people are proud to accomplish. When a culture of acknowledgment and appreciation exists, your helpful assessment of potential areas of growth will be valued.

Effective leadership is a complex set of interactions where many critical skills are required to be effective—the ability to acknowledge is one, and a powerful one often overlooked. As Executive Leadership Coach Harriet Nezer eloquently told me in an interview: "Leaders who make full use of acknowledgment find that it is one of the most powerful tools in the arsenal of influence skills. Acknowledging people fulfills a core need—the need to be known and appreciated for who they are."[3]

Acknowledgment and striving go together. When people feel validated through acknowledgment, they can't be stopped. They will bend over backward, working massive amounts of overtime or going to great lengths if necessary to get the job done the best they possibly can.

When we push past our limits, we make a profound impact in other people's lives. Ultimately, life and work are all about our actions and how they are received. Acknowledgments make us thrive—they give life to our spirit. There can never be too many of them if they are authentic and deserved. And you as a Grateful Leader can find those opportunities to generously deliver them every day.

Chapter 10

When Employees Feel Valued, They Stop Playing Hooky

Principle #6:
Acknowledgment improves physical and emotional well-being.

There is much scientific evidence that gratitude improves overall well-being, alertness and energy, diminishes stress and negativity, thus boosting the immune system. This causes us to believe that when Grateful Leaders acknowledge others, it has similar effects on them, and greatly improves their well-being and sense of purpose. It also improves your own health and well-being to lead in this way.

Gratefulness, an inward-felt and articulated acknowledgment, has long been heralded as a virtue essential for health and well-being. It turns out that acknowledgment and gratitude are not just beneficial for your team and coworkers but also for your own well-being, alertness, and energy. In the article "In Praise of Gratitude," published in Harvard Medical School's *Harvard Mental Health Letter*, *gratitude* is defined as "a thankful appreciation for what an individual receives, whether tangible or intangible. With gratitude, people *acknowledge* the goodness in their lives."[1]

In fact, current scientific research supports the fact that acknowledgment and gratitude are healthy for both the giver and receiver. Dr. Martin E. P. Seligman, a psychologist at the University of Pennsylvania and one of the leading researchers in the field of positive psychology, conducted a study in which 411 people were asked to write and personally deliver a letter of gratitude to someone whom they had never properly acknowledged for their kindness.

The results showed that participants' "happiness scores" increased significantly. And, most importantly, he noted that the benefits lasted for a month. This study had the greatest impact of any positive psychology interventions he used.

The description on Amazon.com of Harvard professor Tal Ben-Shahar's book *Even Happier: A Gratitude Journal for Daily Joy and Lasting Fulfillment* is as follows: "In this week-by-week guided journal, Tal Ben-Shahar offers . . . exercises to inspire happiness every day. Using the groundbreaking principles of positive psychology that he taught in his wildly popular course at Harvard University, . . . Ben-Shahar has designed a series of tools and techniques to enable us all to find more pleasure and meaning in our lives."[2] The role of gratitude in creating a happier, healthier life—and I would carry this over to both the Grateful Leaders and to the recipients of their gratitude—seems indisputable!

Research now suggests that gratitude also allows people to better deal with stress (causing them to be more optimistic), which seems to boost the immune function. According to positive psychology research, gratitude increases people's level of happiness and positive emotions, and it improves health (as also noted in "In Praise of Gratitude" in the *Harvard Mental Health Letter*[3]). Interestingly, one of the studies on gratitude and well-being concluded that high levels of gratitude can even promote better sleep![4]

Another study has shown that "grateful people experienced less sleep harming negative cognitions, and more sleep promoting positive cognitions, which seemed to explain why they had better sleep overall."[5]

So if you want a good night's sleep, make sure you are expressing your gratitude to the people around you for their gifts, talents, and contributions!

A few more facts to build the case for Grateful Leaders' practicing gratitude and appreciation: research now suggests that gratitude offers a great number of health benefits. For example, more than 12 studies have supported the fact that gratitude is linked with subjective well-being and it is closely connected with mood and life satisfaction.

A 2003 study conducted by University of California psychology professor Robert Emmons and University of Miami psychology professor Michael E. McCullough focused on the effects of gratitude on physical and emotional well-being. The study concluded that people who practiced gratitude rated their lives more favorably and experienced fewer symptoms of physical illness, such as stress and fatigue.[6]

"If you want a strategy to increase your happiness, there's a lot out there that will help," says Emmons. "You can take pharmaceuticals like Prozac. But gratitude is something that doesn't have side effects."[7]

Since gratitude is both the state from which a person acknowledges another and the grateful response of the recipient, these findings should apply to acknowledgment as well as gratitude. Here is where the fifth C, Commitment, should enter the picture.

If you are a Grateful Leader, or a leader who sees yourself as being in development, as does the U.S. Army's Brigade Combat Team Chaplain Primitivo Davis, then you make your commitment to feeling, expressing, and acting upon your gratitude. Davis has said this in a way that I find deeply moving:

> I see myself as a "developing" Grateful Leader. I was first introduced to the power of acknowledgment at the most perfect time in the advancement of my professional career. I had just made the transition from being supervised to being a supervisor. During that period of self-reflection needed to truly lead my team of 13 soldiers (made up of chaplains and chaplain assistants), the power of acknowledgment provided me with a great resource to lead in a spirit of acknowledging my team.
>
> I will always categorize myself as a "developing" Grateful Leader because I personally believe that you can never be grateful enough, and you can never acknowledge enough. The discipline of acknowledgment and gratefulness is a lot like my golf game . . . I can always do better! Being a Grateful Leader to me means that each day I am thankful for the privilege to lead others. It means that I use my sphere of influence to better individuals, who in turn better others, which in turn betters the world![8] (See the complete profile of Chaplain Davis in Chapter 12.)

You can't say it much better than that! And I sincerely believe that this Commitment is what brings health and well-being to the thousands of soldiers that are touched by Chaplain Davis's gratitude and who then touch others. Engagement of employees is at least in part a function of their feeling appreciated and valued, so it is no wonder that a Gallup Survey done in the United Kingdom shows this logical but still astounding fact:

Wellness/Productivity Impact

- Gallup study—engaged employees in the UK take an average of 2.69 sick days per year, while the disengaged employees take 6.19. Sickness absence costs the UK economy 13.4 billion pounds annually.
- Engaged employees are more able to handle workplace relationships, stress, and change, which boosts productivity, missions accomplished, and their well-being.

Are they truly healthier when they are engaged and feel appreciated, or are they feeling an overall sense of well-being from this that makes them want to be at work much more of the time? Either way, it's a good result.[9]

I met a Brazilian woman at a conference who, after working 12 years in information technology, was diagnosed with breast cancer and began undergoing difficult treatment. This involved occasional absences from work, but she didn't tell her supervisors the truth, afraid that they would let her go.

When HR finally called her six months later, her fears were realized. HR fired her, claiming she was no longer able to do her job. Out of work for a year, she grew increasingly despondent until one day when a friend asked her to send him her résumé. Then she got a phone call that changed her life.

A businessman was calling to ask her to come meet him for an interview. With trepidation she agreed, expecting more rejection.

But it turned out that their interview was very comfortable, and he treated her with the utmost professional respect. When he asked her about her cancer, which she had cited as the reason for being let go from her last job, she told him it was in her breast.

"Well, it's not in your brain. So it won't interfere with your work," he said. "Why don't you start immediately?" This person had acknowledged who she was apart from her illness, and the results have been astounding: not only is she thrilled with her job but she has also been able to discontinue several of her medications, since her cancer has gone into remission.

Is this an example of cause and effect? That's hard to prove, but we do know that her new boss's actions and acknowledgments had a tremendous effect on her sense of well-being and perhaps her overall health as well.

I know that, in my own life, I have experienced this as well. As a juvenile diabetic, I managed the challenges of the disease quite well, going on an insulin pump, testing my blood sugar 10 times a day, and doing much more. But without a doubt, the negative, perfectionist attitude of a previous doctor had me so frustrated that my self-care was not the best I knew it could be. I felt defeated. When I changed doctors 15 years ago to one who consistently acknowledged all of my efforts (Dr. Donald Zwickler) and who told me that I was doing a great job in terms of managing the disease, my confidence soared and my care deepened. Each time I go now for my quarterly checkup, I anticipate and look forward to the acknowledgment and cheerleading I know I will get (which I do believe I deserve even when things are not perfect)—and yes, I depend on it and flourish from it.

Being recognized and acknowledged for my capabilities, rather than chastised for my imperfections, encourages me. This cheerleading capacity is a critical one for leaders at all levels. It speaks to the ability to motivate and influence others. Often leaders have difficulty knowing how to motivate and influence those with whom they have to work and who are necessary for getting a project accomplished, but over whom they wield no authority. This capacity to identify opportunities for acknowledgment, to make the Choice and engage in Communication to acknowledge, can be a powerful tool in these kinds of instances.

In my case, it had a life-altering effect. In fact, I received a medal from a major diabetes research institution, the Joslin Diabetes Center, "for 50 courageous years with diabetes." What an acknowledgment and victory that was for me! Sometimes courage is what it takes to be the people we are meant to be. I know that I can travel anywhere in the world to speak about my work ("have mission, will travel") and deal with the challenges this kind of travel presents to the management of my condition, because I am grounded in my own capabilities to manage it all, even when I am a bit fearful.

Grateful Leaders who practice authentic acknowledgment, like caring and positive medical professionals, can make people feel and act and perhaps even be a lot healthier, more inspired, and certainly courageous.

It is now known that recognition and acknowledgment release dopamine in the brain, a powerful, feel-good chemical that creates pleasure and a desire to repeat the experience. In a Gallup management journal article entitled "In Praise of Praising Your Employees: Frequent Recognition Is a Surefire—and Affordable—Way to Boost Employee Engagement" by Jennifer Robison, the author referred to this result as the "dopamine drench" that people receive when they experience appreciation and praise. According to Gallup, fewer than one in three workers report receiving praise from a supervisor in the last seven days, as measured by the Gallup Q12, a 12-item survey designed to measure employee engagement.[10]

In a 2008 recognition study by Towers Watson, it convincingly states:

> When a manager surprises an employee—and her peers—with unanticipated recognition, the emotional power increases significantly. Dopamine, and the positive mood it creates, contributes to innovative thinking and creative problem solving, both important contributors to high performance.
>
> High performance, in turn, produces the next round of reward and recognition, which gives rise to engagement and innovative solutions to problems, and the circle continues.[11]

Isn't this too cool for words? I love finding the evidence to prove what we all instinctively know! It just confirms that we are geniuses— or even better, we are probably Grateful Leaders in the making!

Without acknowledgment, you may find yourself furious and resentful, saying to yourself, "Why should I do this job if nobody cares?"

But when you receive praise, you can work on the same project with a completely different attitude—with acknowledgment you're more likely to be motivated and energized, and you'll want to do more. This difference could occur in an instant—and it can be better than a raise.

In a post on the Huffington Post's Healthy Living Blog, Michelle and Joel Levey wrote (July 1, 2011):

Both ancient teachings and modern medical research agree that one of the quickest, most direct routes to restoring harmony and balance in our lives is to foster gratitude and appreciation. The moment you shift from a mind state of negativity or judgment to one of appreciation, there are immediate effects at many levels of your being: Brain function becomes more balanced, harmonized, and supple; your heart begins to pump in a much more coherent and harmonious rhythm; and biochemical changes trigger a host of healthful responses throughout your body. Especially in difficult times, remembering to return to gratitude is a radical life-affirming act that builds your capacity for resilience.[12]

Many leaders find it easy to cite negative results achieved by their workers and to judge them accordingly, but few are able to shift into that state of gratitude and appreciation that not only energizes and lights up their workers but also gives these leaders a sense of well-being and fulfillment. All leaders seeking to maximize performance, retain their best employees, and increase the bottom line should be aware of this: stressful emotions (such as those that are created when people feel deserving of praise from their leader but never get it) produce an excess of a neurotransmitter called *epinephrine*.

Research in the field of psychoneuro-immunology has indicated that an excess of epinephrine causes a chemical breakdown, resulting in the weakening of the immune system and an increased potential for disease.[13] Wouldn't any concerned and caring leader think a dose of gratitude resulting in praise and appreciation of the employee was worth it if it were deserved?

For years Dr. Rolland McCraty has been going so far as to say that appreciation and other positive emotions lead to alterations in the electrical activity of the heart that, in turn, may be beneficial in treating high blood pressure and in preventing sudden death in patients with congestive heart failure and coronary artery disease.[14] Now that's worth paying attention to! Grateful Leaders will see this simply as further justification for their existing modus operandi of letting people know how much they matter and what a huge difference they make!

If I seem to be going on and on with the research findings (I feel a need to reach the left-brained people, as well as the right-brained people like me), let me return to what I know and love best: the stories that prove that Grateful Leaders make a difference, using the power of acknowledgment—and a huge one!

Here's a story of a surprisingly delightful man who used this power for years as part of his job, at the time as the assistant chief of the Brooklyn South Borough, New York Police Department (NYPD). He was later promoted to chief of the transit bureau, NYPD. And anecdotal evidence has it that his people take fewer sick days, and they have a great sense of well-being and lower stress levels, even though they engage in a highly stressful kind of work.

During a workshop on the power of acknowledgment for the U.S. Department of Justice as well as representatives of various federal and state agencies, someone from a New York State agency said that he had met a real master of acknowledgment in his career and that the person's name was Joe Fox, and he was the assistant chief of the Brooklyn

South Borough. Others seemed to know him as well, and heads were nodding in agreement. I filed the name away for future reference.

Shortly after this, I led a similar training workshop for 30 executives in the New York Police Department, and again the name of Chief Joe Fox surfaced. This time just about all heads were nodding in agreement, and everyone seemed to know him as a "Master of Acknowledgment." Example after example of his gentle, far-reaching skills were cited. This was becoming serious—I really had to put Chief Fox on my "must meet" list.

Then I went back to the NYPD to train another group of executives. This time, one of the NYPD executives came up to me and suggested that I autograph a copy of my book for Chief Fox—he was sure it would mean a great deal to him.

Captain Sosnowik, whom you have already met and who is the commanding officer of the Leadership Training Section, agreed wholeheartedly, and he said he would make sure the book got to the chief.

A few days later I got a heartfelt message of thanks for the book on my voicemail from the assistant chief of police and a suggestion that we get together at some point to share our desire to change the world for the better. Since then, I received a beautiful poem from Chief Fox that I have gotten his permission to share with you. He wrote it after visiting a number of hospitals, watching nurses make momentary, yet infinite "differences" in the lives of vulnerable people, when they most needed them. Acknowledgments, too, allow us to be "messengers of grace" and to help the world. The chief saw that similarity immediately after receiving the book, so it is indeed an honor for me to share Chief Fox's vision with all of you:

Help the World

In our lives, we see so many people in pain, in need

many of whom we cannot help

making us feel powerless

unable to make a difference

unable to have a meaningful impact in our world.

But every day there are moments,

special opportunities when we can comfort one person

be a messenger of grace

bring a moment of peace.

And when we help another,

"person to person,"

we help the world.

Even for just a moment

—*Joseph Fox, Brooklyn Chief of Police*

I finally had the honor of meeting Chief Fox at an NYPD leadership training session at which he was one of the presenters. I now know for sure that together we will bring these positive messages forth in powerful ways to help the world. And all of us can be among the messengers of grace who do this every day.

Chapter 11

WHEN YOU WANT TO ACKNOWLEDGE PEOPLE, THERE ARE MANY WAYS TO DO SO

Principle #7:
Acknowledgment needs to be practiced in different ways.

Develop an acknowledgment repertoire that will help you reach out to the people you lead in the different ways that will be the most meaningful to each person individually. Your gratitude creates the context in which all of this can occur most powerfully.

Acknowledgment needs to be practiced in different ways, depending on the needs of the recipient. That's why it's important to develop an acknowledgment repertoire that will give you the tools to reach out to people in your organization or on your team and to other stakeholders in the unique ways that will be the most meaningful to each situation and person.

For example, I have the kind of relationship with the CEO of my company that breeds deep and meaningful acknowledgment—not lightly given, but always truthfully and in a heartfelt way—that both of us remember for years. I gave her one that was carefully thought-out and considered, following the first global on-site sales meeting our company ever held, which brought together our managing directors and members of our Global Corporate Council from IIL companies around the world. It was an amazing event, and I felt extremely proud of the vision it had taken to make this happen, as well as the outstanding logistical accomplishment and creativity.

Although I had to talk to myself a bit about the advisability of acknowledging my boss in a profound and heartfelt way (even after 20 years of working together, I still worried a bit about whether she might think I was brownnosing, manipulating, or being a suck-up), I overcame my concerns because the acknowledgment was burning inside me and needed to be expressed. So I wrote this e-mail to my boss:

Dear LaVerne,

At the global sales meeting last week, it was almost beyond belief to see managing directors, business development managers, and general managers from around the world, all gathered in New York City, to share their challenges and their triumphs with all of us. I felt incredibly proud . . . to be part of this global team. I felt (and continue to feel) extreme admiration of you and of your vision for what this company can be and become. This has guided and directed us to the place we are today. I am truly awed by the way in which you spot and seize the next opportunity, far ahead of the marketplace, and make it a success. I know, for example, that IIL Media is one of those opportunities. The investment of time and funding is certainly a challenge to you and to the company, but that doesn't stop you from taking action and moving forward. Those actions are courageous in an uncertain economy, but they always seem to work out. That was the case with our e-learning initiative just after 9/11, because we were poised and prepared to make the necessary changes, having made the investment in the software platform the year before.

In all, the sales meeting was a totally professional, exciting, motivational, inspirational experience. . . . Thank you for knowing it was the right time to do this and for putting the time, energy, funding, and commitment into making it awesome. Once again and always, I am honored to be part of IIL and to have been on board since its beginnings. I am honored to have this ongoing partnership and collaboration with you. May it continue to bring about positive and worthwhile initiatives and successes to IIL, and to the world.

Warmest regards,

Judy

Her simple response moved me deeply, and it let me know that I had not overstepped or that it had been taken the wrong way. I realized how great a need our leaders have for acknowledgment and gratitude from us, as well as the other way around. Here is what she wrote:

Hi Judy,

Thanks very much for taking the time to put your many thoughts into this e-mail. They are much appreciated. And, by the way, I have all (or most) of these special notes that you have given me over the years . . . in one of my many keepsake books.

Now onward together to see what we can "get into" in the year ahead! Always a pleasure having you close by.

ELJ (E. LaVerne Johnson)

I got teary as I discovered that she had been saving my acknowledgments—that they truly meant something to her. I hadn't known that, and I felt honored and proud. And yes, when the spirit moves me, as I am sure it will, I know I can do it again without fear of negative repercussions.

In a culture of appreciation, such as the one we work hard to achieve at IIL, I do believe acknowledgment is contagious. On the day I received the note from my boss, thanking me for my heartfelt acknowledgment of her and of the company, I read a note from one colleague who works at our global distribution center in Missouri to another colleague in New York. It was so heartfelt and pure that it made me profoundly proud of the people who have chosen to be in the company I have worked at for over 20 years. Here is what she said to that colleague:

> I have been with IIL for five years in June, and I have not met a kinder person than you. I have never heard you say a bad word about anyone. I have only heard kind, appreciative words from you. I want you to know, I appreciate you and I only hope someday to be as kind and thoughtful as you.
>
> In short, I think you're a wonderful person, and I hope you have a beautiful day!
>
> Respectfully,
>
> Wendy

It was clear that Wendy truly "got" who her colleague was. Even if the recipient's overactive brain can come up with countless exceptions to Wendy's statement of acknowledgment (that she never heard her say a bad word about anyone), she can realize that overall this is true. My guess is that she will work on it even harder now, in order to live up to Wendy's generous and heartfelt assessment of her.

A while back, I heard an enchanting example of a way to acknowledge a team member. One woman apparently was full of so much positive energy that she somehow managed to light up everyone on the team. At the end of the project, she was given a set of sparklers. She was told that she was so animated and vibrant on the team while working on the project that she totally deserved this symbol of her brightness and aliveness. She was thrilled with the gesture, and she will undoubtedly remember this acknowledgment forever.

Companies can show their appreciation of their people in many different ways. "Our people are our single greatest strength and most enduring long-term competitive advantage," says Gary Kelly, CEO of Southwest Airlines.[1] While these may sound like just words to many of you, Southwest speaks freely of the "love" of its employees and their customers that translates into wonderful story after story about how both groups truly feel "loved." This entry on the Southwest Airlines website seems to say it all, and then some:

What's LUV?

Southwest has been in LUV with our Customers from the very beginning. Therefore, it's fitting that we began service to San Antonio and Houston from Love Field in Dallas on June 18, 1971. As our Company and Customers grew, our LUV grew too! . . .

With determined Employees issuing tickets from our "Love Machines," we changed the face of the airline industry throughout the 1970s. Then in 1977, our stock was listed on the New York Stock Exchange under the ticker symbol "LUV." Over the ensuing years, our LUV has spread from coast to coast and border to border thanks to our hardworking Employees and their LUV for

Customer Service. . . . We don't take our commitments lightly. We are dedicated to doing the right thing, we take great strides to ensure your safety, and fostering trusting relationships between our Employees, our Customers, our Suppliers, and our Planet.

Wow! Don't you just LUV it? I do believe that a shorter word for *acknowledgment* is *love*, so it is likely that this is practiced across the board at the airline. It is also clear that in addition to acknowledgment, it takes commitment to outstanding performance and, in this case, to true service in order to help an organization like this one thrive.

Southwest Airlines was one of the few that did not suffer dramatic economic setbacks during the downturn of the last few years. Harris Interactive reported this on April 10, 2012:

Among the Value Airlines, Southwest Airlines soars above the rest of its competitors as this year's Harris Poll EquiTrend Brand of the Year. Jet Blue ended up in second place.

Even as Southwest has evolved into a major national carrier, it maintains its original "sassy" brand character and continuously creates a unique atmosphere for its loyal flyers. That "spirited" brand character, coupled with bucking the nickel-and-diming trend, has created a passionate and devoted following.[2]

Who wouldn't be passionate and devoted when the basis of the brand is love!?

You, as a Grateful Leader, have the power to enliven, engage, inspire, motivate, and keep your best people by acknowledging them for who they are and what they contribute to your organization. Your gratitude, if authentic and heartfelt, will reach into the deepest places in your people as well as in your own soul. They will know it in an instant, if you truly feel it and want to Communicate it to them. Don't worry about embarrassment or about discomfort—yours or theirs. And don't worry about whether they might think you are trying to get something from them.

You are—and it's their best selves, their best performance, and their true gifts and talents. They will only respect, appreciate, and honor these efforts that you make to display the deep sense of gratitude that you feel.

In the answers to the questions we used in her profile in Chapter 12, one of our Grateful Leaders, Lynn Batara of Franklin Templeton Investments, described the different approaches that leaders can take to personalize and customize acknowledgment to be most meaningful for the recipient. She describes how she was able to creatively craft acknowledgments that met both the individual and group needs of her employees:

> One of the most important things I've learned is that different people respond to different types of acknowledgment. I tailor the way I show my appreciation for employees based on who they are and what's important to them. For example, I might take one person out to lunch and we'll chat about work, maybe even about things going on in our personal lives. Other employees might not desire or value that kind of interaction, so instead I might send a short e-mail letting them know that I appreciate how much of themselves they put into their work. Other people respond well to gaining new responsibilities or more visibility to other departments or leaders. However you do it, the most important thing is to let them know that they are *special* and *valued*.[3] (See the complete profile of Lynn Batara in Chapter 12.)

Letting people know you believe in them and in their strengths, those that they may not even be aware of themselves, is another powerful way to acknowledge them with longlasting effect. Here is just such an account by Steven DelGrosso, PMP, director of project management competency for IBM's Project Management Center of Excellence. It makes this point powerfully.

I've had a long and very enjoyable career with IBM . . . 34 years and counting! I've worked in several business areas of the company and managed many employees since I was first appointed to management in 1984. Recently I received a phone call at my home office from a woman who had been an employee of mine back when I first became a manager. She has not been employed with IBM for many years, but took the time to look me up in our public directory. The purpose of her call was to thank me for giving her an opportunity to move from our manufacturing area to our engineering team, way back so many years ago. She thanked me for recognizing her talent and expressing confidence in her at that time when, early in her career, she was looking for growth opportunities. She also told me that my coaching and encouragement had influenced her career from that time in a very positive way. You can imagine how energized I was by that phone call, knowing how events that transpired almost 30 years ago were a continuing positive influence on another person.

So Steven's story clearly and dramatically demonstrates how none of us can ever know how profound an effect our acknowledgment can have upon other people, shaping their careers and even their lives, as his did. Don't waste a single chance to make this kind of difference!

Take a moment now and consider the following list of people that you as a Grateful Leader might acknowledge and what you could say to them. Think about the person you are acknowledging: would a written response be more comfortable than a face-to-face Communication? If the latter, should it be public or private? Also, what do you want to say not only about the person's superb efforts, but also about the impact that the person's behavior or performance has had on others?

You can notice how people have grown, how their efforts have helped others and affected not just their colleagues but your customers, your community, or even the planet. Understanding what has meaning and value for them can help your acknowledgment be more personal and therefore more impactful.

For example, everyone in my company knows that the way to my heart and the greatest acknowledgment I can receive is to know about a customer whose life has been changed by reading the book or taking our course "Leadership and the Power of Acknowledgment." Now here are some of the people you can reach out to with your acknowledgments and gratitude:

- Boss (See the example earlier in the chapter, if this category makes you uncomfortable.)
- Subordinate 1
- Subordinate 2
- Subordinate 3
- Coworker 1
- Coworker 2
- Coworker 3
- Mailroom assistant
- Office manager

- Client 1
- Client 2
- Washroom attendant who keeps the place sparkling clean
- Janitor (I heard about a senior leader who, when he has trouble figuring out the solution to a problem, finds the janitor and tells him the problem in simple, understandable terms, and almost without fail, the janitor comes up with a new idea for a solution that the leader hadn't considered before. So don't forget the janitors!)
- Customers whose communications to your organization have led to positive changes and improvements
- Suppliers whose reliability and quality standards are unquestionable
- And anyone else you can think of!

You have unlimited opportunities on a day-to-day basis to share your gratitude with your people for who they are, what they contribute, and for the fact that they have chosen to work with you and your company. Don't worry about showing too much gratitude. If it's real, it's perfect and can never do any harm. I don't say that this state of gratitude comes naturally to all leaders. You may need to access it and remind yourself that your people can choose to work anywhere.

It is an honor that they have chosen to work with you. Your letting them know that in a variety of ways will make them want to stay there forever and keep contributing, in bigger and better ways. And don't forget the high cost of losing employees and having to replace them.

Your Grateful Leadership, if it is authentic and heartfelt, can prevent these losses in many cases. These are pretty powerful incentives for wanting to keep your best people engaged and happy. They can enhance your own personal sense of gratitude for the opportunity to lead and bring people to their fullest potential.

You as Grateful Leaders can truly have an impact on the health, well-being, and capabilities of hundreds, thousands, or even millions of people. What you bring forth in a state of gratitude will touch not just the people who work with you, but also the people they touch— their families, their friends, their communities. Your gratitude makes a huge difference to people. They will feel known, valued, and appreciated for your acknowledgment of who they are and what they contribute. I wish you a wonderful, gratifying and enlivening journey, and I acknowledge you for reading a book on such a groundbreaking subject as Grateful Leadership.

That you have chosen to learn more about this exciting way of leading others says a great deal about who you are and what you are personally up to. It is much more commonplace for leaders to expect gratitude than it is for them to feel it and use it to engage, motivate, and inspire others. As you go through your days, your nights, and your planning cycles and project deadlines, it will help if you touch base with the 5 Cs:

1. *Consciousness:* Remember to be or become Conscious of the acknowledgments and gratitude already present for you.
2. *Choice:* You next need to choose whether to deliver the acknowledgments or to merely keep them floating around in your mind.
3. *Courage:* It will always take Courage to deliver a heartfelt and authentic acknowledgment. If you feel that you need to summon up your Courage, you know you are on the right track!
4. *Communications:* The easy part is figuring out the best way to reach your recipient. There are unlimited ways to do so.

5. *Commitment:* You will find it hard *not* to commit to this form of
   Grateful Leadership, once you witness the benefits to your people
   and how they come alive, want to take on more, and work with
   passion and engagement.

Since you have read this book, I know you are up for the challenge
and that you will make your working environment a place in which
people can fully express themselves and their passions and their desires
to make a difference. Good luck!

Now let me introduce you to the outstanding Grateful Leaders
who I had the honor and the pleasure to interview and interact with
in order to bring forth the essence of their commitment, their style,
and their authenticity. You will feel like you know each one personally
when you are finished reading their profiles, and I know you will find
each to be an inspiration as you move forward on this path.

In subsequent chapters, you will also have the opportunity to do
some exercises and create reflections that will help you implement or
enhance Grateful Leadership. You will see how acknowledgment exists
(or doesn't exist overtly) in other cultures. You will also read some true
stories (mini case studies) of acknowledgment that were contributed
by people I greatly respect. You will have the opportunity to "listen in"
on some amazingly profound and inspiring acknowledgments contributed by participants in my classes, which I hope will inspire you to take
similar actions.

So now let's continue on this exciting and energizing path that
guides us to being or becoming fully realized Grateful Leaders.

PART 3

GRATEFUL LEADERSHIP IN ACTION

Chapter 12

GRATEFUL LEADER PROFILES

PROFILE 1—LYNN BATARA
ENTERPRISE PROJECT MANAGEMENT OFFICE DIRECTOR
FRANKLIN TEMPLETON INVESTMENTS

To me, a Grateful Leader is someone who brings out the best in others, someone who believes in others when they don't always believe in themselves. Grateful Leaders give people the support they need to persevere and grow, cheer them on along the way, and celebrate their successes.

I believe that people see me as a Grateful Leader, and this is based on what they've said to me or communicated through e-mails, cards, and even instant messages! Over the years, I've saved meaningful cards and e-mails in a "warm-and-fuzzy file" at my desk, and on the off chance that I'm having a bad day, I'll thumb through the file. It completely turns around my mindset! Simply being reminded that I'm appreciated makes me feel ready to tackle any challenge that comes my way. And this warm-and-fuzzy file wouldn't be possible if I didn't acknowledge others myself!

When I tell people that I appreciate their hard work and the tremendous results they produce, more often than not, I can tell that it really touched them. I just get filled up with positive energy because I know that I made a difference in their day, and this feeling gives me more energy to go about *my* day! This positive state allows me to look at things from the standpoint of opportunity and possibilities, and it makes me want to create a similar experience for the next person whom I connect with that day.

One of the most important things I've learned is that different people respond to different types of acknowledgment. I tailor the way I show my appreciation for employees based on who they are and what's important to them. For example, I might take one person out to lunch, and we'll chat about work, maybe even about things going on in our personal lives. Other employees might not desire or value that kind of interaction, so instead I might send a short e-mail letting them know that I appreciate how much of themselves they put into their work. Other people respond well to gaining new responsibilities or more visibility to other departments or leaders. However you do it, the most important thing is to let them know that they are *special* and *valued*.

I try to show my staff the same kind of support I've been given throughout my career. I've been blessed with great bosses and mentors who saw my strengths, got to know what was important to me, and made or found opportunities for me to succeed. They made the time to provide me with feedback, praise, suggestions, and advice, all with different approaches, but producing the same result: making me feel energized and inspired because people believed in me.

Sometimes that's all people need—a little reminder that they are appreciated and that their role truly matters and does not go unnoticed. I facilitated a large-scale project closeout meeting with a project team that had worked together for about three years. I felt grateful that they had invited me to be a part of their team for the two-day session, and I was inspired by how close-knit they were and all that they had accomplished.

I really wanted to find a way for the group members to remember what a great experience they had working together and be able to take a little bit of that culture with them to future project teams. I gave all of the team members a blank piece of paper and had them write their name at the top. Then we passed these papers around the room, giving everyone the chance to write something that he or she appreciated or would remember about each person on the team. It was reminiscent of signing yearbooks in school—there was a lot of laughter!—and this continued until everyone received his or her own page back.

The team members enjoyed reading their page, and it served as a meaningful memento of their time together (much more so than would the typical trinkets or logo items that usually commemorate projects).

I had an opportunity to attend Judy's "Leadership and the Power of Acknowledgment" workshop at the Society for Human Resource Management (SHRM) Talent & Staffing Management Conference in San Diego. During one exercise, Judy asked participants to write an acknowledgment of someone in their professional lives, and I chose a former boss whom I had worked for on and off for about 15 years. As I reflected on all that I wanted to thank her for, I was so overcome with gratitude for the positive impact that she had had on my career and in shaping who I am, that I starting crying right then and there!

After I wrote the acknowledgment, I couldn't wait to give it to her (it's not very often that you get excited about giving someone a thank-you note!). Later, I received a note from her telling me that she really treasured the acknowledgment, so much that she would pay it forward with her own staff. That's the most wonderful thing—when you acknowledge the importance that a person has had in your life, it motivates them to do the same for others.

As a Grateful Leader, I value the opportunity I have to express this gratitude to the people I lead and to those who lead me.

PROFILE 2—ROBERTO DANIEL
SENIOR DIRECTOR, ENGINEERING, QUALITY AND CONTINUOUS IMPROVEMENT, SOUTH AMERICA
INVENSYS CONTROLS, BRAZIL

I grew up in São Bernardo do Campo, Brazil, where I would play soccer with other children, some of whom were very poor and lived in slums. I learned to give value to everything I had—like my treasured Matchbox cars, which I kept into my adulthood in hopes that I would someday hand them over to my children. I now have two kids, Pedro and Marco, who along with my wife are my reason for being.

My family has always inspired me. My maternal grandmother is the inspiration for my gratitude in life and in work, as she was a World War II survivor and emigrated with her children (one of them my mother) from Italy in the 1940s. She taught me to treat all individuals with respect and courtesy, regardless of their walk of life. She taught me to greet people with warmth and to always say "thank you," "good morning," and the like. Even as a child I knew the importance of these simple words.

I learned to see people as people, for who they are and what they have to offer—not as an ethnicity, economic class, or occupation. And this is something that I've carried with me all of my life. I apply these same values to my work, and I am continually looking for ways to show my coworkers and peers that I am grateful for the things they do.

One way I've acknowledged my teammates is through a formal initiative called the "Candy Box Awards," which honors them for their contributions and unique talents. I speak about their achievements in front of the whole team, and I present them with a box of candy and an inspiring book (very often Judith's *The Power of Acknowledgment*, Jim Collins's *Good to Great*, or James Hunter's *The Servant*—in Portuguese). The ceremony is documented with photos, which are saved to the company's intranet and sent to the entire management team. I'm happy to say that this initiative was well accepted at Invensys and has become an official procedure!

Years ago, I set out to acknowledge one of my quality leads at the time. While he was faced with managing a chaotic supply base, I saw that he was able to endure many stressful challenges with his forthcoming, empathetic nature. I scheduled a group meeting and announced that we would be acknowledging a certain colleague for his achievements. When I announced this person's name, there was a sudden burst of applause—it was clear that I was not the only one who felt he deserved this recognition. The employee was filled with emotion, completely taken by surprise (and I confess that I too blinked back tears, and I was moved by and deeply appreciative of his positive response).

When I show gratitude and appreciation for my coworkers, I truly mean it. Doing so does more than boost morale and motivation. It builds something even more powerful: trust. I am able to be a great

professional because of the people I work with—because of their contributions and because they help me grow as a person and a leader. In
fact, since 2005 I've requested my own 360-degree assessments, which
are typically not given to executives. I welcome and value this feedback
because it helps me to continually improve, and even more, because it
comes from people whom I sincerely appreciate and respect.

PROFILE 3—XAVIER JOLY
GLOBAL DIRECTOR, PEOPLE DEVELOPMENT
VOLVO POWERTRAIN

I have moved from country to country throughout my life—France to
Sweden, then Belgium, and now the United States, where I have lived
and worked for the past two years. At Volvo's Hagerstown, Maryland,
facility, I experience a feeling of real gratitude every single day, and I
spread it around by spending as much time as I can with my people. I
feel that it is my job to empower them, engage them, and raise their
self-confidence, and I do this through acknowledgment. This can
mean anything from a smile, to involving them in the decision-making
process, to providing coaching and support, or just simply and truly
listening to them. Dedicated, active listening is one of the truest forms
of acknowledgment because it expresses so much in such a simple act;
it is as if you are telling the speaker, "You matter."

I truly value my people's opinions, and I make sure they know that;
however, there are times when, in order to help your employees, you
need to disagree with them! For example, I launched an initiative—a
school in Volvo Powertrain, focused on project management. I told
20 senior project managers that I wanted them to get their Project
Management Professional® (PMP) certification in three months, and

I assured them that they would have all the knowledge and support needed to pass the exam, as well as a commitment from their top managers. They fought me, saying they needed six months to prepare, but I was adamant in my belief that they could pass the rigorous exam in only three—and 90 percent of them did! I think they felt that "the company believes in me, so now I have to believe in myself." It worked!

Since I was a teenager, I've loved being on a team. At the risk of sounding pretentious, I was the captain of every sports team I belonged to! But it wasn't because I was the greatest player. It was because I was driven to lead. I had the energy and ability to instill confidence within my teammates and make them challenge the impossible. And although I was the leader, we only achieved things as a team. Playing on French national teams, I had a choice of handball versus triple jump (collective team versus individual sport), and I chose the team.

I once spent time coaching an individual to help him find a needed solution, even though he was not a direct report of mine. I told him that I wasn't the expert, but he was, and that I knew he would make the right decision. The people on his department team came to me and said that even though I wasn't their manager, they were ready to do anything for me. They said, "We believe in what you say since you let us do what we wanted, but only if it was in the right direction." This team was very special to me, and I let them know. I had to "learn" them since they were from the United States, and I came from the French culture—but they were the ones who were lacking confidence!

Take the time to recognize and acknowledge your people's competence and their ability to find solutions, and you will see how much it energizes them. When you exhibit the trust you have in your people, you will see that it drives them to deliver even greater results than expected because they are *fully engaged* and eager to create success for the team, the company, and for you. Do not forget that people are making the difference, and as a Grateful Leader, you can help them achieve amazing things.

Profile 4—Michael E. Case

President and Chief Executive Officer
The Westervelt Company

A Decatur, Alabama, native, I began my career in the packaging industry when I joined Gulf States Paper Corporation in 1981. Over 30 years later, I'm still the first person to recognize I have achieved more in my business career than I ever expected. When I reflect on how I arrived here, however, my thoughts are filled with lessons I have learned from influencers and that I seek to share with others as we continue this journey.

My parents were great role models for me. I experienced appreciation every day. I liked how it made me feel. So it was easy for me to treat others the way I wanted to be treated. While I had many positive role models growing up, I think of my maternal grandmother when I think of gratitude. She was the oldest of 11 siblings. She was the foundation of that very solid family. She knew everyone in town because she worked as a clerk for the city water department. Back then, people paid their water bill in person.

She knew when people were in need, and more often than not, she reached into her purse when "help" was needed. She had little financially, but she appreciated everything. She took nothing for granted and never missed an opportunity to thank others. She was the kindest person I have ever known, and when I consider her actions now, I see two behavioral dimensions that were not apparent at the outset: optimism and patience. It takes courage to share what little you have, but doing so communicates that you believe resources are renewable, and you continue striving until they have been replenished.

A Grateful Leader is focused on others. Gratitude implies appreciation, and to fully appreciate others one must be genuinely interested in people. It means having trust in the competence of others along with an honest assessment of one's own strengths and weaknesses. I believe Grateful Leaders have a low sense of entitlement and high sense of personal accountability.

My achievement in business can be directly linked to this understanding of servant leadership, and this is often validated by my colleagues through their positive feedback. As a result, our company has formal programs (financial rewards and public recognition) that highlight associates' contributions in the areas of safety, continuous process improvement, and cross-selling. Additionally, the company's leaders have gone a step further to include servant leadership as one of the key behavioral areas in their annual performance measurement. Informal recognition through private and public praise, as well as personal handwritten notes, also helps promote an environment of acknowledgment and appreciation.

There is no doubt these programs have raised productivity. When I am about to hire someone who will play an important role in the company, I take them out in a social environment—not to entertain or impress them but to be able to pay careful attention to the way they treat people who can do nothing for them in reality—the waiters, the the people bussing tables, the hostesses. How they treat those people is a certain reflection of who they are and who they will be in our working environment.

It's really an age-old secret: simply treat others the way you want to be treated. Be intentional in your actions, and forgive yourself when you fall short. Find something about each person that you engage with that you can appreciate, and tell that person in a very specific way about what you found in them. Gratitude and how we as leaders show it is a very important and much overlooked aspect of leadership.

PROFILE 5—CAPTAIN DANIEL E. SOSNOWIK

COMMANDING OFFICER LEADERSHIP TRAINING SECTION (LTS)
NEW YORK POLICE DEPARTMENT (NYPD)

The day I was to be interviewed by Judy for this book, I was honestly feeling terrible. It was a bad day from many perspectives, and I was, in truth, lacking the very thing I had been asked to speak about. I told my story as best I could, and after our 20 minutes focused on gratitude, I found that my entire perspective had changed for the better. Our conversation became a staunch reminder that when a person is focused on being grateful, there isn't any room left in his or her mind to stew in negativity.

For some, constantly having a positive perspective comes naturally, but I really had to learn it from scratch. I met people who were grateful in their lives, and from them I learned to be more grateful in mine. These were spiritual, not necessarily religious, people who appreciated life and understood the importance of being the best person you can be. I'm still so thankful for those who taught me, and as commanding officer of the Leadership Training Section (LTS) of the NYPD, I try to transfer these same values to the people I teach, to my colleagues, and to those I interact with day to day.

I've been with the NYPD since 1984, and I've worked a number of Christmases over the years—I'm Jewish so I'm happy to do it. On one Christmas several years ago, I made an announcement over the dispatch radio: "I want to thank all of you for all of the work you do all day. Have a great holiday, and get home safe." Then I told the dispatcher, "By the way, Central, this also goes out to you and everyone behind the scenes. Thank you for what you do." The dispatcher's voice cracked. There was a complete outpouring of responses as a result of this communication, and it really resounded with me.

I don't know how many of my colleagues remember that, but the power of this story is not just in acknowledging the officers (that is, taking 15 seconds to break with tradition by using our radio to convey a truly personal message) but also in the emotions that overcame the dispatcher, because I believe she realized my thanks indicated that she and her colleagues weren't just voices—they were as much a part of our police family as the rest of us. Truly, our radio dispatchers are the unseen voices and the unsung heroes. Wherever an officer is on any given day—but especially when he or she is, heaven forbid, shot or fighting for his or her life and screaming for help into his or her radio—it's the dispatcher who makes a difference by calmly managing radio transmissions and guiding his or her colleagues to their location. It is often the difference between life and death.

The idea of dealing with people as people is the key to my definition of a Grateful Leader. All people deserve to be acknowledged and appreciated for not only the things they do but for who they are—you acknowledge the person, not just their act. There is a human need to be treated as a person of value. Simply put, people want to be treated as people—not as a "number" being talked at—and this applies to the classroom environment as well as the community we serve.

Since 2006, I've designed training and development curricula for NYPD supervisors, middle managers, and executives. When you are in front of a classroom, the most important thing you need to do is make sure you are connecting with the people, as I've found that our students learn best when they're part of the discussion. Their active input is encouraged, appreciated, and in fact, *needed* in order for the instructor to have a truly successful class. As we know, leadership also requires training competencies, so we therefore include the conceptual framework of sharing information and eliciting feedback as the model for our supervisors to use with their own subordinates.

In a regimented, hierarchical organization (as is common in law enforcement), people tend to be very conscious of rank. However, although rank is significant, I am a firm believer that thinking and working as a team—instead of focusing on individual authority— is much more beneficial. Thus, we ensure that our students come away with the understanding that what is successful in the classroom environment can easily be transported into their interactions with their subordinates.

I'm fortunate that my duties also take me out on patrol twice a month, as a "duty captain." I travel throughout one of the patrol boroughs of the city (in my case, Brooklyn South), visiting precincts, reviewing conditions, responding to large-scale emergencies, and conferring with supervisors. As my tenure here at LTS increases, I come into contact with more of our graduates, and I'm gratified as more and more of my students remember me from their time in our programs. I always take a few minutes to "pick their brains," looking for information regarding their own experiences, and I explain that the information they share may serve to help me further update our curriculum back at the academy and address current concerns. As always, they are involved—just as they were during the actual training. Few things make people feel as good as knowing that their opinion is sought and valued.

Excellence deserves praise and acknowledgment, and leaders must always remember that. As a new captain in 2002, I was called to the scene of a particularly gruesome car accident, involving a fatality. It was late at night, raining heavily, and the scene was awful. Yet the sergeant who handled the accident was so thorough, so professional, that I spent a few minutes that morning preparing a report acknowledging his good work under some of the most difficult conditions. I forwarded the report to his commanding officer and to the head of his bureau, as well. He called me shortly after to thank me for my acknowledgment. And then I didn't see him until some six or seven years later—I didn't even recognize him at first—but the first thing he said was another profuse thank-you to me, for taking the time to recognize his performance on that difficult night. Such is the power of acknowledgment.

PROFILE 6—JANIS O'BRYAN
CHIEF INFORMATION OFFICER
HUDSON ADVISORS

I have been the CIO at Hudson Advisors for 15 years. I am fortunate to work with such a talented and committed team of professionals. To me, being a Grateful Leader means appreciating, supporting, and respecting my global team. I see myself as a Grateful Leader because I understand that my team is responsible for my success and I couldn't do it without them. I am naturally a grateful person due to my humble upbringing on a farm in Kansas as a middle child of four where we had food but other resources were limited. I remember as a small child, I would get two pairs of shoes a year, and they had to last. This humble start led to how I appreciate the opportunities in my life. I have deep gratitude toward those who have helped me along the way. My experience has shown me that if people feel appreciated, they do their best work. I do believe that people see me as a Grateful Leader based on the fact that I have high retention rates with my team. After 15 years with Hudson, I still have my first hire on the team.

My gratitude influences my leadership style and strategy as I strive to foster recognition programs within my group, reward teamwork, ensure that training is available to my team, and always maintain a budget for their development and performance bonuses. I have implemented six-month reviews rather than just annual reviews so that there is a focus on goals and my staff's development. I give special rewards inside the group to recognize teamwork and initiative. These awards are given based on nominations from peers or others in the company.

I work to keep my team growing by rotating the leadership of staff meetings each month, which gives team members a chance to develop their public speaking skills and also gives them a chance to be seen as a leader inside our area. I do extensive research to make sure my staff is paid appropriately in the market and are incented to achieve their bonus potential. I feel it is also important to take the time to send appreciation e-mails (and courtesy copy peers) and to celebrate birthdays and anniversaries by mentioning specific contributions of that person. I try to do small things like bringing in food for no reason other than to celebrate the day. I also have one-on-one or small group lunches with team members to give them time to have my undivided attention to share ideas and talk about their life.

Last year, I created the global Center of Excellence (CoE) where skills are detailed for each role to clearly define each team member's span of control globally and expand on their defined responsibility. Through the CoE effort, I also developed a skills matrix so that we could manage a much needed, global task consolidation effort within Hudson. The company is moving away from decentralization of IT to centralization in the Europe, Middle East, and Asia (EMEA) market, and the CoE supports this initiative by utilizing the existing talented staff regardless of their location. This helps protect their jobs regardless of the changes in the business direction.

I performed an employee satisfaction survey a few years back. One of the results of that survey was a request for better corporate communication, which resulted in a corporate intranet that my group implemented and maintains. One of the feedback points the executives heard is that as a global company, their employees needed a place where they could collaborate, and so the intranet was born.

I dedicate time to network with other professionals and make time to give back to my community. Through this effort I have built lasting relationships with other Grateful Leaders as we understand the importance of giving selflessly. The effort to improve the lives of others is a reward to all involved. I feel that by mentioning and celebrating specific accomplishments of our employees during birthday and anniversary celebrations, I am fostering a culture of gratitude.

By giving my time and attention to ensuring the continued professional development of my staff members, by meeting with them one-on-one or in small groups, I'm empowering them to share their ideas and have "face" time with the senior leadership of Hudson. Finally, by having those sessions off site, the employees feel comfortable to be themselves and share openly. By giving them my time and attention, I am also giving sincere and heartfelt acknowledgment.

Being a Grateful Leader is just a part of who I am as a person. This is a difficult topic to put into words, but I see being grateful as a willingness to do anything I might ask my team to do. I'm not afraid to roll up my sleeves and pitch in when I'm needed because I've worked my way up the ranks. I feel competent to pitch in and do any task I might ask the team to do. I can be truly grateful because I have done what they do each day.

PROFILE 7—PRIMITIVO DAVIS
BRIGADE CHAPLAIN
THIRD BRIGADE COMBAT TEAM (3BCT)
TENTH MOUNTAIN DIVISION, U.S. ARMY

I see myself as a "developing" Grateful Leader because I believe that you can never be grateful enough, and you can never acknowledge enough. The discipline of acknowledgment and gratefulness is a lot like my golf game. . . . I can always do better! I was first introduced to the power of acknowledgment at the most perfect time in my professional career. I had just made the transition from being supervised to being a supervisor. During that period of self-reflection needed to truly lead my team of 13 soldiers (made up of chaplains and chaplain assistants), the power of acknowledgment shaped my belief that a Grateful Leader must be thankful for the privilege to lead others. Being a Grateful Leader means that I use my sphere of influence to better individuals, who in turn better others, which in turn betters the world.

Earlier in my life, my gratitude toward others was elicited only by "great" deeds, so I have consciously worked to develop an appreciation for the "little things." Leadership experience has taught me that gratitude spread out over time for the little things is more effective than infrequent doses of gratitude for great feats. The little things often serve as a foundation for great accomplishments, so why value them any differently? For example, soldiers are often officially recognized through the Army's award system. Awards are conferred based on combat contributions, unit contributions, distinguishing events, or time in service.

Although Army leadership seeks to award all soldiers fairly and equitably, it is inevitable (as with any award system) that sometimes people are missed, or they feel as though they deserved a higher-level award or recognition. As a chaplain, when I perceive such sentiments,

I would seek out the soldiers who may have been disappointed and acknowledge them for their contributions. Although their total value and contributions may not have been recognized in the form of an award, their impact on combat operations, particular events, the unit, and our nation was equally as powerful.

Just as heroism exists on a small and large scale, the expression of gratitude can be just as impactful in a sincere "Thank you." Many soldiers shy away from official awards for our sacrifices, but the most simple and moving acknowledgment we could receive is the handshake of a stranger in Walmart. With this in mind, my Grateful Leadership style integrates casual and formal means of acknowledgment. I write a personal handwritten note to one of my team of 13 each week telling that person what I appreciate about him or her either professionally or personally. Then, during the four times a month that I formally brief my commander, I use at least one of those times to highlight one member of my team. Such a highlight is not traditionally part of my brief, but I have added it to my brief based on an intentional attempt to be a Grateful Leader.

I know that my team is only as strong as the sum of its individuals, so I have a number of tools in place to assess, foster, and acknowledge the strengths of each of them. One of these tools is my "Profile Book," a three-ring binder that contains a profile of each of my team members. Each profile contains the individual's current résumé, biography, family information, and long- and short-term professional goals. However, the most important part of the profile is a collection of surveys that seek to identify personality traits. Although I don't rely on these tests to label or simplify my team's characters, I find them helpful in identifying people's strengths and illuminating how they are "wired."

My role as a teacher, coach, mentor, and trainer is then developed based on the unique gifts of the individuals on my team. I concentrate mostly on the positive aspects of who they are, and I tell them that this will be the foundation of our team. I do spend time developing them in "weak" areas, but the split is about 80/20—80 developing and using their strengths and 20 developing the other areas.

My ever-improving sense of Grateful Leadership is inspired by the unfortunate childhood memories of not being appreciated myself, and the desire to do better by my team. By intentionally and systematically acknowledging individual members of my team, I hope to create a professional work environment conducive to acknowledgment and gratitude "up," "down," and "across" the proverbial ladder.

This is my motivation: Grateful Leaders will produce more Grateful Leaders. I am 1 person, but I lead 13. If I can produce 13 Grateful Leaders who subsequently produce 13 Grateful Leaders when they are promoted, then I will have created 169 Grateful Leaders . . . and so on. That is how the world is changed for the better, one person at a time, and that first person has to be me!

Profile 8—Walter Robb
Co-CEO
Whole Foods Market

Gratitude is a wonderful word. It makes you stop and think: to whom and for what am I grateful? Have I displayed my gratitude, and if not, how can I do so? Focusing on gratitude brings an emotional awareness of others to the foreground and propels you to examine your own consciousness. Both personally and professionally, gratitude has played a huge role in my life, and it only continues to help me grow.

When you love what you do and the people with whom you work, you have reason to be grateful. When your business is built from the passion and creativity of your team members, you have reason to feel blessed. Once I was struck by the insight that those who work with me make it possible for me to do what I love, I became a stronger leader. In fact, every new breakthrough that helps me to listen to and collaborate with my team helps me grow a little more. And I can lead only to the extent that I have grown as a person.

The real core and secret of Whole Foods is belief in people. When I do store walk-throughs, I don't just "walk through." I spend two to three hours there and ask myself, "Do I feel the spirit? Are team members happy?" I have learned to ask questions rather than give orders because the more I can uncover, the more we can do as a company. I hear people's stories and create space for them to feel acknowledged. A particularly moving suggestion for change came from a customer on behalf of her blind son. The young boy wanted to experience grocery shopping at Whole Foods too. So a marketing team member in one of our Los Angeles stores created Braille tags to be put into three departments. Once this was done, the young boy had the opportunity for a Whole Foods Market experience. Whole Foods has built, and continues to build, a culture in which people feel listened to, valued, empowered, and respected. This results in a constant percolation of new ideas and continued movement in the company.

I don't know that I would have walked through stores this way 10 years ago. But I do remember now a turning point for me. At 22, I had my own natural food store. One day I mentioned to one of my cashiers, Laura, that I needed a truck driver. "My husband Hank might be willing to help," she said. I didn't think that much of it until Hank showed up at the store at 9:00 p.m. with a lunch pail and thermos. I thought, "Wow, I have a responsibility to him. He took my offer seriously."

As a leader, I knew where I needed to go, but Hank taught me that we need to go there together. I realized that I had just as much of a responsibility to him as he had to me. When leaders truly join their teams in this way and acknowledge the greatness of each individual, they connect the head and the heart of their business, thereby breathing life into it.

I recently gave a talk at Washington State University, which was titled "Toward a More Sustainable View of Business: A Retailer's Perspective." I've developed a sort of ritual that I carry out before I give any of these talks. I close my eyes and remind myself to focus on three things: *gratitude, humility,* and *giving.* Be grateful for the opportunity, be humble about it being a team effort, and make sure to focus on giving to this group. Focusing on this makes me feel centered because I am reminded why I am really there. It's not about me. It's about empowering people by truly believing in their talent and individuality.

As a leader with a strong sense of purpose, I work to create an organization of empowerment by believing in my team and then pushing them to follow through on their talent. In the past, my determination led me to use heavy-handed tactics and actually take power away from those who worked with me, but I am learning to give others space and inspire them to work hard and take responsibility. My drive has not waned, but I have grown and matured enough to embrace healthier methods of inspiring team members. Instead of being overwhelmed by my responsibility to thousands of team members, I see the potential for greatness in the free working of all those minds, and I encourage individuals by raising the bar.

As a leader at work and as the single father of three children, I have learned that gratitude naturally stems from acknowledgment of people's talent and creativity. So while I can still be intense, I am also trying to be caring and grateful. Leadership requires a constant recalibration of how to be true to one's personal drive and still be true and open to others.

At Whole Foods, our master script is, "We believe in the potential of our team members." I love bringing natural food to the world, and I believe deeply in the people who make it possible. In my career, I have learned how truly amazing other people are. I realize this on deeper and deeper levels all the time. I think of the amber waves of grain from the patriotic song "America the Beautiful," and this brings forth an image for me of "unfolding waves of gratitude."

Gratitude is and should be ever unfolding, revealing always deeper levels of gratitude that we carry with us as we walk in the world. It is always more enriching, and there are always more layers. This image of unfolding waves of gratitude reminds me that I can be grateful for every opportunity that I am able to identify, to serve my team members, my customers, their communities, and the larger world of which they are a part. This is a big, thrilling, and challenging job. It is one that I am honored to hold, one I am committed to carrying out to the best of my current abilities, and for which I am committed to developing new abilities that can help me even better meet these challenges as they present themselves.

(*Note:* This profile consists of excerpts from an audio interview conducted with Walter Robb in March 2012.)

PROFILE 9—TOM LAFORGE
GLOBAL DIRECTOR OF HUMAN AND CULTURAL INSIGHTS
THE COCA-COLA COMPANY

Viktor Frankl once said, "Success, like happiness, cannot be pursued; it must ensue, and it only does so as the unintended side effect of one's personal dedication to a cause greater than oneself." This quote exemplifies a new shift in corporate thinking that I'm working to bring about, and it represents the mission the Coca-Cola Company and I have undertaken with people and organizations outside the Coca-Cola System in an effort to enrich the global community within which our company operates. I am grateful for Coca-Cola's commitment to moving in this direction as we build outward to promote what it is that causes people to feel better about themselves, to feel happy, contented, and in the broadest sense, well.

Coca-Cola, like many corporations, is evolving from a product-focused model of business to a human-focused one. Getting to know people more deeply and completely is my mission and the mission of the Human and Cultural Insights Department, which I head. That my job is to lead and inspire many of these efforts with heartfelt human insights is something for which I am deeply grateful. In fact, I can hardly believe my good fortune.

Several years ago, I created a new department at Coca-Cola with the enthusiastic support of my boss, Stan Sthanunathan, vice president of marketing strategy and insights. We both had spent over a decade conducting consumer research, but every year the feeling that we were not quite getting at what really mattered kept getting stronger. I came to the conclusion that what mattered most was twofold: human nature, itself, and culture.

Human nature was what I really wanted to study! What are our eternal drives and motivations, our life stages, fears, hopes, and dreams? What are the biological and physiological truths about us that propel us to seek hydration, nutrition, social connection, and recognition? The cool thing about human insights is that they are universal and timeless. We can apply them to our business in every one of the more than 200 countries in which Coca-Cola operates. We can share them with our bottling partners, our retail partners, and our community partners.

Human insights unify us because they are about us, about what every one of us shares. No matter how big the world seems to be, we are, in the end, united by the simple, singular truth that our human-ness, not what we drink, is what really unifies us.

We are creating an energized business atmosphere where people in our company are grateful to be working on such meaningful issues because their focus reaches beyond themselves, beyond the corpora-tion, and out into the heart of the community. I have a dear friend and Coca-Cola colleague in Istanbul, Fatmanur Erdogan, who works with me on our Every Drop Matters partnership with the United Nations, an effort across 12 countries to bring clean drinking water to people without. When I was with her last month to hear reports from each of the program managers, one story in particular touched and inspired us both.

It began with a young woman from Sri Lanka. She looked like she could have been a friend of my daughter's—late teens, early twenties, perhaps. And yet she routinely faced a simple decision that nobody should have to make. It's the middle of the night and you have to pee. Your only option is to venture out in the dark moonless fields where young women run the risk of being horribly victimized. No longer was I thinking of stats.

I was trying to imagine what it must feel like to lie awake with her fear and discomfort as she tried to decide what to do. I imagined what a mother must feel when she hears her daughter head out into the darkness. As a father, I've lain awake many times waiting for my daughter to come home. Late at night, minutes can pass like hours as your imagination generates scary possibility after scary possibility. But never did I have to worry about something like this.

Bringing indoor toilets to these few women (our project is a modest one) didn't just deliver convenience, health, and sanitation; it helped one girl, one mother, and one father to sleep a little easier. For the remainder of that day, I would hear report after report about toilets or clean drinking water. But it was the image of one young woman being able to sleep peacefully that made me grateful to work for a company with the resources and the conviction to help.

We, all humans, are part of a large interconnected network. Thriving in a networked world requires new rules that define how people can support, nurture, and help each other. When the focus shifts to supporting others, gratitude becomes instrumental in forging positive relationships. Simple techniques of expressing gratitude spread quickly. Every time somebody from my team speaks to a group, we acknowledge at least two people who helped us. This becomes contagious, inspiring more people to express gratitude for others, which creates solidarity and human connection among colleagues. With heart-led leadership as a foundation, it is easier and more natural to translate consumer data to individual human lives that we can positively impact.

Recently, I shared these views at Hasbro. A few weeks later a box of Hasbro's best toys and games arrived at my house as a thank-you. And nice as they were, what really made the toys and games valuable was that for one brief moment I got to hear the excitement in my teenage son's voice as he opened up the box while I was at work. I was on the other end of the phone as he unpacked the box, becoming as excited and giddy as the happy nine-year-old I remember him as. You see, he's been having a pretty tough time lately, and this was a moment, maybe not two or three minutes long, that I valued more than any amount of money they could have sent me. Why? Because my son was happy.

Capitalism is evolving, and so are corporations. This evolution happens only when the people running corporations feel the need to update their views of what it means to be a good company, a good businessperson, and a good member of an interconnected world. For corporations to thrive, communities and the planet must thrive. It is the outward focus of supporting others that I love, and this is exactly what my Office of Human & Cultural Insights exists to do. While the responsibility of my office is a macro one—ensuring that the global Coca-Cola Company thrives in the years ahead by keeping apprised of global trends—I believe real change must start on a micro scale: the individual.

Remember how Frankl explained that success and happiness flow from our dedication to a cause greater than ourselves? This "greater than oneself" orientation is what Abraham Maslow discovered at the top of his famous pyramid. All the happiest, most successful people he studied, people he called "self-actualizing," had this outward orientation.

I often share this concept of selflessness as a key to success in the emerging new world. This might not fly in a lot of offices, but it works at Coca-Cola, the company that naively but authentically proclaimed its desire to "teach the world to sing." There is an egalitarian ethic woven into the core of the Coca-Cola brand that gives permission to such ideas. As I see it, humility, kinship, and respect are the secret formula for all companies wishing to thrive in our interconnected world.

Working at Coca-Cola allows me to improve communities around the world, advance my personal journey, and help my colleagues do the same. The wonderful part is that, as we strive to achieve any one of these three goals, we find we simultaneously achieve the other two. Being the best outward-oriented person you can be leads to personal happiness, business success, and thriving communities. And for this opportunity, I am truly grateful.

PROFILE 10—MARK ADDICKS
CHIEF MARKETING OFFICER
GENERAL MILLS

The Grateful Leader taps into one of our most fundamental wants: to be recognized as an individual. In a world that upholds efficiency over meaningful interaction, the Grateful Leader's approach is uncommon, simple, and powerful.

We all want to know that we are making a difference, and I think the basic belief that you can change lives for the better—that you can make a true difference in how people see themselves and what they can contribute—is the starting point for being a Grateful Leader. If you have this belief, then by nature, you will engage everyone on a deeper level and create an environment that others want to join.

Of course, there are studies that say a more inspired team, wherein everyone feels appreciated, listened to, and moved to contribute, is usually higher performing. I believe we all know from personal experience that this is true; we tend to be more committed to the whole of the business when we feel our role is valued. But I think there are some things that these studies can't tell us. Can a study explain what it feels like to be truly acknowledged for who we are and what we have to offer? No, we can only experience that for ourselves.

Today I lead our centralized marketing services and resources, which is a diverse group of functions including digital and social media, promotions, and content, plus stand-alone operations like Boxtops for Education and Plateful, a digital food advertising and content network. I am directly responsible for over 200 individuals and their careers, but I know that the degree of informal trust and individual influence that I foster is far more important than any job title. As our challenges are solved person to person, with shared thinking and creativity required, the practice of Grateful Leadership is critical. Whether I am talking to a creative lead at one of our advertising agencies, trying to find that one idea that can ignite the brand, or sitting face-to-face with buyers at a major retailer, convincing them to partner on an idea in their store that must deliver "the numbers," it is the level of trust and authenticity that wins the day.

I think informal recognition is the best and most meaningful way to acknowledge others. And although there is a time and a place for plaques and ceremonies, I have always deeply appreciated when someone took the time to send me a note to say "thank you" or acknowledge something I did.

Recently, I received a handwritten note from someone who was retiring from my organization. In it, she said how much she had enjoyed working for General Mills, but she said that what was even more important was that I had made her time with us a growing experience because she felt constantly challenged to do more and learn more. This was powerful for me, and it was the best present anyone could give.

Another large part of Grateful Leadership is being tethered to those around you. It's having a balanced sense of self, accepting that there is much more beneath the surface, and recognizing that sharp judgments are often a dangerous way to lead. I have learned many times that we do not realize the extent to which people will put aside their own trials and tribulations when in the workplace. It is always humbling to find out in conversation that someone has a loved one struggling with a disease or a family challenge at home, all while contributing at a high level at work.

Not long ago I was invited to brunch by a social friend, and she mentioned that her sister, a student of mine over 15 years ago, would be attending and was excited to speak with me. My class was her sister's favorite throughout all of college, my friend said, and she had even gone on to be a teacher because of it! I was embarrassed because I couldn't recall who she was, but I immediately remembered her face as soon as she walked in the door. We talked for well over an hour about the class, her life since, and her teaching experience. It was a firm reminder of the potential power that every teacher—and leader—has to make a positive impact.

My grandfather was a farmer and lifelong schoolteacher, and for all of my early years I would run into people in our small Texas town who, after learning my name, would proudly tell me that he was their teacher and how they had learned so much from him. I have been fortunate enough to experience incredible examples of gratitude from many gifted people in my life, but the strongest example has undoubtedly been my family. My parents, now in their 80s, volunteered and helped others from my very first memories.

One time in particular, a local family was struggling with cancer and having trouble making ends meet. My parents took the whole family in to live with us until they were back on their feet. I was a teenager and less than pleased at the inconvenience this caused, but it is one thing that I have remembered and learned from my whole life.

For me, Grateful Leadership is not an "end state"; it's more of a commitment to a state of being. Grateful Leaders strive to find the best in others (and in themselves), recognize the role and contributions of every individual around them, and acknowledge that Grateful Leadership itself is a constant journey.

Growing up, I saw how my grandparents were active in their communities and how they treated everyone with respect. They had gratitude for what they were given in life and believed the best way to express this was by helping people in their own quiet way. From them, I learned how simple acts of acknowledgment could eliminate so much negativity in life. They guide me even today to remember the importance of making a human connection with everyone with whom you come in contact. I don't always do it, and I am certainly not perfect, but I try every day to stay true to their example.

PROFILE 11—KIMBERLY SUPERSANO

CHIEF MARKETING OFFICER

PRUDENTIAL ANNUITIES

While traditional leadership roles see the leader as the shining star, Grateful Leadership is as much about the followers as it is the leader. In fact, I've found that the roles of leader and follower are very much intertwined.

Transitioning from an individual contributor to a leader of people created new challenges for me. In the workplace, it's easy to get caught up in "trying to get the job done," but as my responsibilities grew, I realized I couldn't do it all on my own. I needed to gain buy-in from followers and find a way to inspire people to want to contribute. I think a lot of people who move into leadership roles have trouble with this. From the onset, they know that people depend on them, but it may take them longer to discern that they, too, will depend on others just as much.

One of the first things I did in my current role was conduct one-on-ones with every employee who now reported to me, all 80 of them. I asked them what they hoped I could help facilitate and what they would not change. I also got to know them as individuals, discussing their interests, their families, and lives beyond the workplace. It gave me a cultural sense of what needed to be addressed and a sense of each person's strengths and passions.

After I conducted the interviews, I held a department meeting to share the themes I had aggregated, and I began with the things that people valued most. Many people said they felt they were working in silos and there was lack of communication and cooperation across the department. This feedback prompted me to create four new working teams (employee feedback, event planning, communication, and employee development) with the purpose of helping to address these topics. Employees volunteered to participate, and I intentionally assigned nonmanagers to lead each group so that they could learn what it was like to influence a team. I think it's equally important to challenge employees to go outside of their comfort zones as it is to support them in their own endeavors. I am a strong proponent of giving people opportunities to capitalize on their strengths, even on ones they didn't know they had.

In my first year, I met with the team leaders once a month to discuss their goals and progress, but it was really up to them to formulate the business plans for their teams and decide how they would add to the work environment. The communication team came up with the idea to create a bimonthly newsletter for the department, replete with personal profiles, an event calendar, articles, fun facts, and interviews. The event planning team organized activities for almost every holiday, many of them including employees' families. We've had summer clam bakes, Easter egg hunts, Halloween trick-or-treating . . . our events have helped form the glue that brings people together and that also allows them to contribute in unexpected ways. For example, the person who photographs all of the events is a systems engineer, but his passion outside of work is photography.

The impact of these working teams was overwhelmingly positive. Employees felt more valued, more engaged, and more willing to help each other. After my first year in my role, I decided to hand-write a letter to each of the department's employees, reflecting on the past year and what we had accomplished together. I personalized a few paragraphs in each letter to express my gratitude for all the unique contributions the person made and to acknowledge how he or she had grown. Over the weekend, I hand-delivered the letters to each person's desk, where they sat waiting until Monday morning. I'm happy to say that many of the employees still have their letters tacked to their cork boards. It's a little reminder that not only do I believe in them, I also rely on them.

I'm also grateful to be part of a company that considers talent development a top priority. In fact, the company's leadership competencies include a commitment to embracing employee talent and facilitating leadership. Outlining such things in a document is one thing, but truly living them through dedication and commitment is another. I am so glad to belong to a company that shares my values and believes in its people as much as I do.

Chapter 13

"Knock Your Socks Off" Power of Acknowledgment Exercise for Leaders™

I n many of my classes I use a special exercise to give people the direct experience of creating and, hopefully, later delivering a profound acknowledgment to someone in their professional career. If they want to go back to their first boss or mentor, that is fine. If they want to acknowledge someone currently reporting to them at that moment, that is also fine. Whatever resonates with them and allows them to dip down deep into that vulnerable place in themselves, where true, heartfelt acknowledgments live, is great.

I usually save these exercises for my longer courses, which are delivered both in person and virtually. I like to give people time and space to write all that really lives in their hearts and to not take shortcuts the way most of us do most of the time.

But one day, I decided to try this in a short, one-hour virtual class as well—to give people seven minutes to write their acknowledgments to someone in their professional career. They would be almost "free associating" by typing their thoughts directly into our text chat, rather than writing them out on the fun form I normally circulate for them to write out the acknowledgment longhand (see illustration at the end of this chapter). In that webinar that day I had 105 people from around the world, and as always, I was amazed and delighted by how intimate the space became almost instantly, just based on the topic. The participants were from Canada; Malaysia; Qatar, Belgium; Kansas City; Istanbul, Turkey; London, United Kingdom; Copenhagen, Denmark; Bangalore, India; Mumbai, India; Brazil; Dubai, UAE; Madrid, Spain; Tokyo, Japan; Munich, Germany; and many more countries and states. Quite a few of the participants were leaders or managers.

I was thoroughly amazed by the results that poured into the text chat, once I explained the exercise, its purpose, and the fact that they would not have a lot of time to think about what they wrote. The ultimate intention of the exercise was for them to not only create the acknowledgment but also to deliver it later on to the intended recipient. I knew that this one-hour webinar was about to change the world in the most dramatic of ways, as the people in the class jumped into the exercise. I knew that relationships of many years would be transformed, enhanced, and healed once the statements were written and delivered. So I sat by in amazement as the moving, stirring, unbelievably honest acknowledgments came flying in. When the seven minutes were up, I started reading some of the submissions aloud. What happened then, I am sure, made webinar history. As I read them, and I needed to do this as the text chat is not saved in the archived version of the program which participants are entitled to access after the event,

I was literally moved to tears. So I cried—not once, but twice, and I remained moved throughout.

The stories tended to fall into a few categories regarding what people wanted to acknowledge. These included service above and beyond what was expected; gratitude for support and mentorship, sometimes in difficult circumstances; and acknowledgment for a quality of personality that was particularly meaningful to the recipient. Here are some of the stories people submitted and my comments on each one, organized into those categories.

SERVICE THAT WENT ABOVE AND BEYOND

BORIS R: Tabish, I would like to thank you for your contribution to our recent performance testing cycle. You've done an amazing job coordinating the work and guiding the teams to accomplish this difficult task. I appreciate the fact that you were always available to help, often at night. I also appreciate your input on improving the process so that the next iterations will be done much more smoothly. Thanks for your great work!!!

> *My comments: The sacrifice of being available at night and commenting on the difficulty of the work are noted and deeply appreciated by the Grateful Leader. Boris also commends his engaged worker for process improvement so that things will go better the next time. Simple, clear, and direct. I predict that this will mean a lot to Boris's subordinate, who will be motivated to do as much or more on the next project.*

NIMA D: John, this is to send you a sincere and big thank-you note! Your dedication and commitment on this project have been admirable. The great success on this project could have not been achieved without your contribution. We have a happy client who would like to have you on her future projects! Keep up the good work!

My comments: Nima is letting her staff member know that his contribution was valued and deeply appreciated. She is letting him know that the job couldn't have gotten done without his contribution—something that makes a person feel special, as well as important, essential, and visible. So often I hear that when people are not acknowledged for their contribution, they actually feel invisible. They feel confused—they had thought they were doing a great job, but because they received no evidence of that from their manager, they wonder where they fell short. Nima is letting John know in no uncertain terms that his success was visible and the client was pleased enough to want him associated with future projects. You can practically feel John's pride and the glow that the praise must have caused him. And Nima's gratitude for that contribution is clear and evident.

APARECIDA G: Jonathan, I would like to thank you very much for all the support you have given me since I started in my position until now, being side-by-side delivering with quality and commitment. The customer experience is greatly shown through the results of our pulse surveys. Thanks for going above and beyond expectations consistently in all the projects we worked together.

My comments: Aparecida has generously affirmed the results of Jonathan's support, expertise, and commitment. To strengthen the case for her acknowledgment of him, she references true, documented results of quality and excellence of the work performed that were revealed in a customer pulse survey—a quick and frequent survey tool that can show immediate results. Some people want or need proof that they really deserve an acknowledgment such as this one. So what Aparecida did was document her acknowledgment. Some people need that, so it is always handy to have a few facts to prove what you are praising. Well done, Aparecida!

BILL T: Maria, when I asked if you knew of a link to our group's mission statement, I had no idea that you would print out the mission statement in color and deliver it to my office. This is fantastic. Then I thought how you always go above and beyond to anticipate what else I might need. If we could all serve each other like this, we would be the most productive group in the division. Thank you!

My comments: What Bill wrote to Maria moves me deeply. He gave her a specific and vibrant example of her wonderful character trait of going above and beyond. It could be considered a simple and nice gesture by many leaders, but Bill's gratitude for this quality that Maria brings to his group is evident and open. He makes himself vulnerable by allowing her to know that she is so tuned in to him that she can anticipate his needs and even meet them without being asked. Some people would fear telling another that she knows how his mind works and what his needs are—those that, when satisfied, allow him to be the best he can be. He uses the word "serve" when he says, "If we could all serve each other like this, we would be the most productive group in the division." Service is a true gift an employee willingly gives to an organization. Beautifully said and demonstrated, Bill!

Support and Mentorship Sometimes in Difficult Circumstances

BUDHADITYA S: Hello, Jacob. My heartfelt acknowledgment to you for shaping up my career the way it is today. The way you have guided and handled me during the initial days of my career has helped me build my foundation, which would not have been as strong without your support, cooperation, and constant nagging. Thank you very much!!!

My comments: The truthfulness of this statement makes it extremely valuable to the recipient—your "support, cooperation, and constant nagging" is indisputably honest and humorous. But we get a clear and instant sense of how Jacob has contributed fully to Budhaditya. Nagging, when done with love, caring, and commitment to the person, can be extremely motivating.

NANCY B: To my mentor, you graciously acknowledge all accomplishments and progress, and yet you consistently provide constructive criticism, encouraging people to achieve the highest levels of performance and continuous improvement.

My comments: The balance Nancy brings forth in her mentor creates a beautiful, honest, and generous "package." The recipient will know the acknowledgment is both real and heartfelt. Her mentor has achieved that delicate balance, and Nancy's appreciation will make it clear that this style of leadership works really well for her and undoubtedly for many others. Her use of the word "graciously" is in my mind a way of expressing the gratitude her leader feels for accomplishments and progress. These things are not taken for granted, and when improvements can be made, this too is expressed and taken seriously.

ROBERT W: I can't send the message because the person I have in mind is now deceased. He was a former boss who in one sentence set my entire career. He called me into his office to ask me to deal with a situation. He started to tell me what to do and then stopped. He said, "You know what to do, don't you?" I said yes. He said, "Then I don't need to do anything here. Just let me know if anyone gets in your way." I learned that I could take charge, and from there, I kept taking on more responsibilities and moved up the chain to management. I never got to thank him for that. He died from cancer a year after that conversation.

My comments: As I read this acknowledgment to our audience, I have to admit that my voice broke. I felt Robert's sadness, frustration, and realization, and this last was what gave it so much meaning for the 104 other people from around the world. How many of us have withheld this kind of simple, yet extraordinarily powerful, statement? A statement that, reduced to its essence, might be, "You have no idea what a huge and positive impact you made on my life in that one moment. I will never forget you. I will be forever grateful." I'm sure that every one of us in that virtual room thought of those we had not fully, profoundly, and generously acknowledged. I do believe that Robert's statement moved each of us to commit to making sure we let those who had made a difference in our lives know about it—as soon as possible. I also suggested to Robert that his acknowledgment was so moving and special, that it could make a huge difference to his former boss's wife, or parents, or children. I know from the painful experience of losing both of my parents in 2008, that when people I didn't even know came forth to find me and let me know, for example, what a fabulous teacher my mother was, it made a huge difference. Therefore I urged Robert to deliver this communication to his boss's family members as well.

JOCK B: M, thank you for believing in me and pulling me back into your organization. When all of the organizational changes were made last year, I felt pushed out and not so important because it was not my decision to move. You came to me three months later and stated that you believed in me and that my skill sets were the ones missing from your organization and had been missing since the move. Thank you for believing in me and providing me with opportunity and pulling me back into the organization where I can maximize value.

My comments: Jock has taken the initiative to acknowledge his manager for an event that was important to him and to his career, that many others would have just said a silent prayer of thanks for—going back to the place he felt he rightfully belonged. How easy it is to overlook such an initiative or just to be silently grateful. I know in my company, our CEO specializes in putting people in jobs in which they truly belong and in which they can make the maximum difference to the organization. Many of us have looked quizzically at her when she has moved someone from sales to a trainer position, or from production into marketing. And then we just watch the person blossom and grow and achieve heights we could not have envisioned. It is a true leadership skill and instinct to know where people belong, and those leaders with that gift deserve acknowledgment—both from the people who benefit directly and from those around them who are witnesses to this gift and talent. Jock's affirmation of the importance of his manager's belief in him is another profound and generous acknowledgment. When a leader truly believes in and is grateful for the talents of a person, the results are a win-win. Jock is now determined to maximize his value in his organization. He has the trust, belief, and commitment of his leader—he will not let him down!

BHASKARRAO E: Manish, I really liked the way you supported and guided me in preparing the project documents and in assigning the challenging new task to me which I had never done before. I highly appreciate the trust and belief you had in me that I will be able to accomplish the assigned task without any failure and to deliver the task on time as expected.

My comments: This is a beautiful acknowledgment of a quality not always found in a corporate setting: trust. Manish put his trust in Bhaskarrao, and this meant a great deal to him. That trust and belief his leader has in him spurs him on to greater and greater accomplishments. It cannot fail to shore him up to know that his manager believes in him. That is what we all want and have to earn. But when we have indeed earned it, we are making our leader "right" and confirming that the trust was deserved. Manish will undoubtedly feel justified in having that trust, will be grateful to Bhaskarrao for earning and deserving it, and trust him on an even higher level the next time. Stephen M. R. Covey quotes Jim Burke, former chair and CEO of Johnson & Johnson: "You can't have success without trust." Trust goes up, down, and sideways in an organization. In this example cited by Bhaskarrao, his manager acknowledged him by giving him his trust, which meant a great deal to him.

MURIEL K: I want to thank you for your support and mentorship. You unequivocally expressed your appreciation when I changed procedures in order to make you feel more secure about the process of the work. This necessitated overriding the feelings of several members of my group, which was difficult for me.

My comments: Mentors and managers need acknowledgment as much as the people they manage. And in general, they are among the most under-acknowledged people in the workplace. Muriel's thanks for her mentor's support will have a positive impact on their relationship. It is also clear that the mentor's expression of appreciation made a big difference to Muriel. It goes both ways, and one feeds upon the other. Muriel also makes it clear that she was able to do that which caused her discomfort, for the good of the process and the relationship with her mentor. Well done!

LISA T: Joe, you have taught me to always do my best and never give up on what I believe in. I have taken this with me through the years. I have watched you inspire others, and I am proud to have worked with you.

My comments: This simple, yet heartfelt acknowledgment, gets right to the point: Lisa's mentor modeled and appreciated her doing her best. Yet at the same time, there may have been areas of nonalignment between them. Even then, she was encouraged to speak her truth and not give up on it. Lisa had that permission to be true to herself and to her values working with this leader. Letting him know he inspired both her and others is her gift to Joe. It is one he without a doubt will treasure and remember, especially when things get tough.

DORIS D: I will be sending this soon, since I have just recently reentered the workforce at a new company: "Thanks for your time during my training and transition into the company. I appreciate your friendly demeanor and patience during this time and that you are always available when I need some assistance."

My comments: How welcome an acknowledgment this would be from a new employee to those that show him or her the ropes! Unexpected, for sure. Appreciated, without a doubt! Many people spend their valuable time training others to fill positions that continuously need new people with different learning curves (and maybe they would need to be filled less often if employees felt valued and appreciated and didn't leave their jobs because they can't continue to work in a corporate culture lacking appreciation). Doris is leading the way in making this happen, and hopefully her example will be contagious—it usually is! And this is a great way to start in a new job in a new company: showing appreciation and not just taking it for granted that she is "owed" training.

SHARON F: To my boss, you have been an example and mentor of how an exemplary senior manager conducts himself or herself on a daily basis. You always treat people with respect and dignity, valuing their opinion and making them feel their contribution is worthy of consideration. You treat people with such fairness, and I truly value you as a wonderful example of how I should conduct myself under all situations. You are a wonderful human being!

My comments: It would seem from Sharon's text that her boss is most certainly a Grateful Leader par excellence. Treating people with respect and dignity, valuing their opinions, and making them feel that their contribution is valued are all signs of such a leader. Sharon remarks on how her boss treats people with fairness and that this is deeply meaningful to her. To a Grateful Leader, rank and status are not factors. People are to be appreciated for who they are and what their contribution is or can be. That is why Sharon so greatly appreciates her boss and closes by showing how much she values that her leader is a wonderful human being. In so many corporations, managers are seen as robots and automatons, with little humanity. Sharon's is one of the ultimate acknowledgments a leader can be given.

ANDREA H: To my former boss, you will never understand how your words of motivation to hang in there and push on made me into the worker I am today. I still call you today just to run things by you even though we do not work together anymore.

My comments: When people change jobs or move on, it is so easy to imagine that they have forgotten the investment we have made in them, the late-night phone calls, and the cries for help, and the wisdom we have tried to impart to them. So now they are gone and hopefully happy and successful. But we have little idea of the role we actually played in their development, in their future. When someone like Andrea comes back to us and lets us know the difference we made, it is an amazing and invaluable gift! While she has kept in contact with her former boss, to run things by that person, she may not have made it clear how much she appreciates the ability to do this before this opportunity to acknowledge someone from her professional career was offered to her. The fact that her boss motivated her to "hang in there and push on" is a great testimonial to that person and to the direction Andrea's career took as a result.

JOCK B: Early in my career, a forklift driver nicknamed "Tiny" was struggling in life and in work. He would make mistakes while driving the forklift and people would yell at him or make fun of him. Tiny was overweight, and the name-calling was awful. I would constantly go to Tiny and tell him he was doing a good job and not to worry about everyone else. In an effort to stop the way he was being treated by others, I tried to make changes, and I had discussions with these other people. One day after work, he came to me and thanked me for always being nice to him. That night he signed his check, gave it to his parents, and went home and committed suicide. He is my inspiration to do unto others as I would have them do unto me. Your words make a difference, positive or negative.

> *My comments: This was one of the entries that had me in tears as I read it aloud to the group. I heard from others as well that had been totally moved by this unfortunate case of what I would have to call basically corporate bullying. In my book* The Power of Acknowledgments for Kids, *I state the following in the chapter called "The Pain of Bullying vs. the Pleasures of Acknowledgment": "In my view, acknowledging is as close to the opposite of bullying as you can get!"*

In schools the world over, educators are trying to combat bullying among students. There are assemblies, workshops; teachers and administrators are trained to step in and do what they can to make the difference. What Jock attempted to do using the power of acknowledgment was to combat the adult bullying and negativity that Tiny dealt with on a regular basis. Bravo to Jock for his commitment, his caring, and his unconditional love. Sadly, though, even this was not enough. My personal thanks to Jock for realizing that the words and the positive actions that he modeled have tremendous power, and for putting this into action. Maybe his telling of Tiny's story will motivate others who hear it or read it to end the kind of brutal bullying Jock witnessed by doing the same. If five people had joined with him to let Tiny know he was a good person and that they knew he was doing his best, would it have saved a life? Perhaps. But as Jock says, all of us need to know that our words make a difference. You, as Grateful Leaders, must choose your words wisely and well. It is your honor and your privilege to do so, and to make sure that others around you are doing so as well.

ACKNOWLEDGMENT FOR THE QUALITY OF WHO YOU ARE AS A PERSON

CHRIS M: Jason, when you speak, your refreshing honesty humbles me, inspires me, and gives me a confidence that comes from your clear direction and simple ease of expressing any problem or issue in basic terms. Your words are easy to digest, yet are so profound and thought provoking. I am so blessed that you consider me not only your coworker but also a friend. Thank you for being you. Don't ever change!

My comments: This acknowledgment is incredibly heartfelt, sincere, and totally moving. When Chris states that he is humbled and inspired by Jason's way of communicating and mentions how his own confidence is heightened by the clear and simple language, we can feel the honesty of it. Chris has demonstrated a real willingness to allow himself to be vulnerable—a generous gift that he is happy to give. Many of us hold back or withhold our generous praise and expression of appreciation of another out of fear of embarrassment or discomfort, or we worry about giving the recipient of our praise the upper hand, and more. Nothing could be further from the truth. All of these withholdings deprive us, as well as our recipients, of our true self-expression, our generous, profound admiration of who they are. Chris was completely willing and able to show that admiration to the maximum.

MARY A: Jim, I appreciate your thoughtfulness and consideration in everything you do for me. I'm blessed to have you in my life. Thank you.

> *My comments: You can't get much simpler than this, but the language that Mary uses goes far beyond what is commonplace and frequently used in the world of work. Her acknowledging that she feels "blessed" to have Jim in her life makes an indisputable statement about how much she values and appreciates him. There is a language of the heart and spirit that is now beginning to enter the workplace. James Kouzes and Barry Posner, for example, in* The Leadership Challenge *have a section called "Encourage the Heart" in which they make the case for recognizing people's contributions. This is where people "live" emotionally—why leave this at home when they come to work? Love and spirit belong in the workplace. They represent our humanity. Feeling blessed by someone's contribution is one of the ultimate acknowledgments one can experience.*

CANDACE C: Mahesh, I would like to take this time to acknowledge the skill set that you have in managing your staff. Of the managers that I have observed in our area, you are the most communicative with your staff members. You keep them informed about information necessary for their jobs as well as spending time with all of them to promote their reporting of their projects and tasks. I truly wish there were more managers with these skills or that would take the time with their staff. Thank you. —Candace C.

> *My comments: This is lovely, clear, and direct. Who wouldn't be thrilled to be held up as a model for communicating with employees? It is generous*

with the list of assets Mahesh has in dealing with his people. Her fervent
desire that there be more managers with these skills is one of the highest
forms of acknowledgment. Candace was kind enough to share with me the
response to her acknowledgment that she received:

> *I wanted you to know that just this morning I followed through*
> *and sent that acknowledgment to Mahesh as well as to his direc-*
> *tor. His director stopped by this afternoon and wondered what the*
> *trigger was for the e-mail. I told her about your webinar and our*
> *"homework." But more importantly, I told her that Mahesh was*
> *an outstanding manager. She appreciated that I had taken the*
> *time to send the note. Thank you again. —Candace C.*

CORA L: To the cleaning lady in our office, I have silently watched you
working hard to keep our restroom sparkling clean for a long time
now. You always greet us warmly when we walk in, but we seldom say
thanks to you. Your kindness and dedication really set a great example
for me, and I wish you to know how much I appreciate it.

> *My comments: How I wish I could get this acknowledgment to people who*
> *use the restrooms in corporations everywhere—in other words, to every-*
> *one! Most of these cleaning personnel nearly faint when we just say "good*
> *morning" to them, let alone acknowledge them for the job they do. I love*
> *how honest and real Cora's acknowledgment of the cleaning lady in her*
> *office is. She states that she has "silently" watched her working so hard.*
> *Aren't many of us also guilty of silence when we see people doing this kind*
> *of work with total enthusiasm and commitment? This kind of acknowl-*
> *edgment, from the ground up, is what helps create a culture of apprecia-*
> *tion within an organization. That Cora planned to let the cleaning lady*
> *know that she set an example for her to follow is a gift beyond measure.*
> *Her acknowledgment is and should be held up as an inspiration to all. You*

as a Grateful Leader can set the example for this kind of behavior and applaud it when you see it!

Now you can try this exercise, using the lighthearted but extremely powerful "Knock Your Socks Off" form below.

The
"Knock Your Socks Off"
Power of Acknowledgment™ Exercise for Leaders

Person to acknowledge in your professional life _____
(Manager, colleague, secretary, team member, etc. If you can't think of a person to acknowledge in your professional life, choose your husband, wife, father, mother, child, favorite teacher, etc.)

What I want to say about him/her (be very specific and write your message to that person)

_____
_____
_____
_____
_____
_____
_____
_____
_____
_____
_____
_____
_____
_____
_____
_____

How I will acknowledge him/her _____
(email, telephone, letter, face-to-face, etc.)

By when I will do it _____
(Day of Week, Date, Year)

© International Institute for Learning, Inc.

Chapter 14

ACKNOWLEDGMENT AROUND THE WORLD

ACKNOWLEDGMENT IN SCANDINAVIA IN GENERAL AND SWEDEN IN PARTICULAR

Guy Grindborg, PMP, is a senior consultant at the International Institute for Learning and holder of Swedish business, marketing, and engineering degrees. He has lived and worked in many parts of the world. His project management background includes customer service projects for Ericsson in Sweden, Italy, Ireland, and the United States, as well as Total Quality Management (TQM) and other improvement projects in many different countries. He developed a corporate project management certification program as well as introduced competence modeling for project, sales, and technical sales. Guy was the operations manager with direct responsibility for 45 integration project managers in the Netherlands. He also has extensive experience from sales, marketing, operations, systems development, technical and professional training (including leadership, performance management, sales, negotiations, project and program management, and coaching).

First of all, let's start with a quick comparison between the three Nordic countries of Norway, Sweden, and Finland *from a Swede's perspective*. (Excuse me, my fellow Nordic brethren, if this isn't the way you see it.)

I have this sense that "feelings" diminish from west to east. Norwegians, I find, are very open and easy to talk to. Willing to share what they think and feel. Easily recognizing a person's or team's success. A great example here is the Lillehammer Olympics back in 1994 that was an enormous success with lots of public acknowledgment in the press and from the government for the contributors. Swedes, well, as one I can say, start buttoning down a bit, some being more open than others.

I will expand a bit on my experience in Sweden later, but let's just say they are the mix between Norway and Finland. Not as quiet as Finns and not as outgoing as Norwegians. Finally, Finns are the quietest and most closed people who do not really like sharing feelings, or for that matter, as Judy wrote in the PMI® Voices on Project Management blog, celebrating each other's accomplishments by acknowledging each other. Her great stories can be found on these websites:

- http://blogs.pmi.org/blog/voices_on_project_ management/2009/06/creating-an-acknowledgement-cu.html
- http://blogs.pmi.org/blog/voices_on_project_ management/2011/01/instill-acknowledgment-into-th.html
- http://blogs.pmi.org/blog/voices_on_project_ management/2010/06/the-courage-to-acknowledge.html

However, as is evident by these blog posts, even the unapproachable and indifferent people will open up when given acknowledgment for their great work or effort.

Let's continue focusing a bit on Swedes since I have more personal experience in that area. We are starting with the Swedish word for "thank you": *tack*. (It sounds like "tuck.") This story occurred many years ago, back in the mid-1980s, when I was working as a technical trainer for a large Swedish corporation. We had a number of students from the United Arab Emirates in training in Stockholm for six weeks.

Within a couple of days they had picked up that Swedes on the street and in the shopping malls sounded like a bunch of chickens. *Tack, tack, varsagod*, with the last word sounding like a rooster crowing, which made them think of a chicken coop. The act of thanking someone for holding a door always resulted in a *tack* or, to show extra gratitude, a *tack, tack*. The word *varsagod*, or "you are welcome," would then typically follow from the person holding the door.

Well, that was then, and this is now. Having left Sweden in the late 1980s for Texas, I find that the act of thanking people in general, and in the workplace specifically, has been forgotten somewhat. A Swedish author, Magdalena Ribbing, in her latest book *Etikett på jobbet—bra att veta på kontoret*, loosely translated as "Etiquette at Work—Good Things to Know in the Office," describes how the word *tack* has almost disappeared from the workplace.

My experience working in Sweden, dating back to mid-1990s, was that the act of recognizing people really drove great performance. My boss at the time, Anders Hellman, made clear to us what his expectations were, and he also held us very clearly accountable for achieving our results. This was a fairly un-Swedish act, holding people accountable, but that is another story. He would spend time with us if we were in trouble, in a positive way finding solutions, and he would recognize us when we accomplished our tough targets by making sure he officially acknowledged our efforts and results.

By the way, our targets year 1 were to double productivity, while maintaining or improving quality, customer satisfaction, and employee satisfaction. His whole management team, of which I was a part, would recognize and support each other during our meetings to meet these tough goals. We, Anders's team, would get together for an off-site meeting every quarter during which we analyzed not our results but how we worked together in teams.

These sessions were always full of high fives for successes and honest and straightforward feedback for where we were flailing or failing. At the end of year 1, we had doubled productivity while improving on all the other indicators. Year 2 goals were to once again double productivity, and yes, we managed even the second year.

Many managers in Scandinavia, and elsewhere, sometimes think that it is unnecessary to motivate people. We all too often hear, "Why do I need to thank them [employees]? They get paid, don't they?" This is a serious mistake. A common trait in our Scandinavian cultures is that of a very strong personality who thinks he or she needs little or no acknowledgment. Nothing could be further from the truth. I have witnessed people who were making a fair contribution for years become great performers just because they were recognized for their contributions.

Many years ago, I inherited an employee from a fellow Swedish manager. He told me: "This guy doesn't want to get his hands dirty. He doesn't do a great job." I interviewed the guy before transferring him to my organization, and I found out that the previous manager had never talked to him about what he was interested in or how he wanted to develop. He had been left as a field engineer for four years with absolutely no feedback on how he was doing his job.

I found out that the guy was ambitious and wanted to learn new things, a perfect fit for my training organization, and so I hired him. He went on to be the technical leader for our newer technologies. I sometimes found him in the lab at the oddest hours, and I had to tell him to go home, of course, after thanking him for his contributions. He sent me a message this year, 2012, telling me I was the best manager he had ever worked for. Great acknowledgment from the person I acknowledged so many years ago.

Finally, I'd like to talk about a good friend in Australia, Rudy Pilotto, with whom I have worked in many parts of the world during my days with a large Swedish telecom company. We trained the leaders at all levels to recognize good behaviors and to provide positive reinforcement and acknowledgment to these individuals. The result was astonishing. One group in two years went from being at the bottom of the heap when it came to software engineering to becoming the third best, out of 17, in that company. Another organization got voted best supplier by the world's largest cellular phone operator after having been trained in acknowledging their people's good contributions. Now all of this of course needs to be coupled with great products, great service, and smooth processes, but the acknowledgment is what starts and drives the journey.

So in conclusion, acknowledgment may not be big in the Nordic countries as such, but when practiced, it shows great improvements in peoples' and organizations' performance. Don't miss a chance to acknowledge your fellow Nordic friends; they do appreciate it, even if they don't tell you they do!

ACKNOWLEDGMENT IN CHINA AND JAPAN

Adrian Dickson is a freelance writer and award-winning journalist with extensive experience reporting and running news teams in Asia and Latin America. During his extended tenure in Latin America, he covered the civil wars in Central America, Argentina's transition to democracy, the Colombian drug wars, and Brazil's economic turnaround. In 2002 he moved to Tokyo where he ran the Reuters news operation in Japan before assuming oversight for news operations for the whole Asia region. Adrian is married with two daughters and lives outside New York City.

Gambaru is the word that Japanese people use to describe their determination to do their best and not give up until a task is completed. At several points in a Japanese life, the spirit of *gambaru* is invoked such as when students sit for their university entrance exams or when university graduates apply to become trainees in their first job in a corporation. *Gambaru* speaks to Japanese doggedness to overcome great challenges and succeed. It also helps explain the Japanese workplace ethic and why Western notions of acknowledgment are so foreign to them.

Japanese employees work hard because that is what is expected of them. Their commitment is not to their personal advancement but to the success of the team to which they belong. They know that, as the popular Japanese expression says, a nail that stands out must be hammered down. It is an adage with which most people in this island nation would probably agree. No one wants to be thought of as that outstanding nail. Japan is a team. It is not a group of individuals. Western acknowledgment styles, praise, or recognition for positive behavior are not something that would normally occur to someone in Japan. They would ask: "Why would anyone need to be recognized for doing something that is right? Isn't that what we are all supposed to do?"

Over much of the last decade I worked as an editor in Japan and later Hong Kong for a major news organization. I am no expert in Japanese or Chinese culture. But my time in Asia allowed me certain insights into the motivations of the people in these countries at a special time in Asia's economic development.

As a foreign manager leading a team of Japanese journalists, my challenge was to obtain the best possible performance from the team of journalists I led, and I did this by attempting to introduce some Western management practices, while not trampling on traditional Japanese values. As a way to encourage greater competition between the newsroom journalists, we launched a monthly Most Valuable Player Award that was given at the end of every month to the Tokyo journalist on our team who produced the best story. The monthly award ceremony was intended to be an animated affair in which the winning journalists would receive a nominal financial prize and a baseball as a trophy.

However, it was obvious that as people assembled for the ceremony, journalists approached the award with equal doses of enthusiasm and dread. While they enjoyed the recognition, their pride was mixed with embarrassment for being singled out for achievement in front of their peers. I was able to get away with this supposedly motivational exercise because I was a foreigner. However, Japanese supervisors who are explicit about an individual employee's achievements sometimes find themselves in deep water. A public expression of appreciation for one person can prompt a negative reaction from others who might question why one person was singled out for recognition when all achievements are the result of the efforts of a team.

Rochelle Kopp, managing principal at Japan Intercultural Consulting, identifies several reasons why Japanese managers are uncomfortable expressing praise to their employees. They do not want to praise work that is not perfect for fear that employees may assume that there is no room for improvement. Managers worry that employees who are the target of praise may take this as a signal that their work is good enough, and that may prompt a drop in motivation. Unlike Western managers who regularly ask their teams to produce significant "step" or "stretch" improvements, Japanese managers believe in a small but steady process of continuous improvement that they describe as *kaisen*. To shower an employee with praise might make her complacent and interrupt the *kaisen* process.[1]

"There is very little (explicit) acknowledgment in Japan. It's not that we don't recognize people, but expressing it is not part of our behavior," said Yuriko Morimoto, a Tokyo-based executive coach and a specialist in cross-cultural communication. She said that instead of expressing acknowledgment, Japanese supervisors are much more likely to criticize the work of their teams. An employee will distill two messages from her supervisor's remark: unless the comment clearly indicates that the work has serious problems, the employee will interpret it as a sign of approval but also that new improvements are in order, explains Morimoto. "Ours is a high-context culture in which people don't communicate things verbally. Even though people might not express gratitude for a favor done for them, you can tell they are grateful from their expression," she said.

This does not mean that Japanese managers do not look for ways to recognize good work. What they will not do is to communicate praise verbally. Messages of acknowledgment are subtly telegraphed in ways that underline the person's value to the corporation and the larger group. For example, a supervisor may invite an employee out to dinner. He or she may not speak about work all evening, but the whole context will speak to gratitude and acknowledgment.

Recognition is also expressed in ways that underline the powerful links between a person's personal and professional life. It is not uncommon for supervisors to be invited to make the main speech at an employee's wedding ceremony. On these occasions the supervisor will extol the person's virtues and his or her loyalty to the corporation. The implicit signal to friends and family is that the employee is highly regarded. Sometimes a supervisor is called to lead a company delegation to the funeral service of an employee's close relative, perhaps a parent or even a grandparent. The supervisor's presence is a sign of the company's commitment and concern for the employee and his or her well-being.

Kopp points out that Japanese managers often wince when they hear Western colleagues describe the work of their teams with superlatives such as "great," "fantastic," or "terrific." She says that it would be completely out of character for them to speak to employees in similar terms. Her advice to Japanese managers who want to offer feedback is that they describe factually what they like about an employee's work and describe what can be done better. This more fact based approach tends to be more comfortable for Japanese," she says.

It is hard to say whether the modern Japanese employee would agree with traditional recognition practices or whether he or she would choose something more personal. After all, travel and modern communications mean that Japan, which is the third largest economy in the world, is no longer isolated from modern global trends. The country's sideways economic performance since the early 1990s has prompted a slew of government programs designed to boost growth, reduce unemployment, and support a clearly stress-ridden population. Social symptoms such as an increase in the number of people who are clinically depressed and peaks in suicide rates have led corporations to offer greater psychological support policies to their employees. There are no statistics to back up the contention that Japanese people are more aware of the need to acknowledge one another. However, anecdotal evidence might well support that view.

In China the concept of acknowledgment is irrelevant unless viewed through a Chinese lens and explained in the context of maintaining "face." To operate in China is to understand that face is at the heart of every relationship. It has sometimes been described as a social bank account because face can be spent, saved, and invested. To take away someone's sense of face is to take away a person's fundamental sense of security. Nothing is worse in the Chinese context than to embarrass or ridicule someone in a social environment. This is as true of personal relationships between two individuals as it is true of the relationship between two families, two institutions, or even China and its relationship with other countries around the world. The repercussions of contributing to someone's losing face can be felt for a lifetime, and revenge should certainly not be considered out of the question.

Face is so central to Chinese culture that it is not surprising that references to it are routine in Chinese proverbs. These include "Men can't live without face, and trees can't live without bark," "A family's ugliness [misfortune] should never be publically aired," or the popular expression "blackened face" as in "He blackened your face to get back at you for something you said." The famous Chinese writer and translator Lin Yutang has said that face cannot be translated or defined. He characterized it this way: "Abstract and intangible, it is yet the most delicate standard by which Chinese social intercourse is regulated."

Foreigners living in China will remark that they will sometimes suddenly find themselves ostracized by Chinese friends, probably because they somehow contributed to their losing face. For a Western businessperson this can be a serious concern. A person admired in the West for being direct and a "straight shooter" would be considered rude and overbearing in China.

In Chinese tradition the practice of acknowledgment has been folded into the annual festival calendar as one of the rituals observed during the Chinese New Year. In this two-week period, which may fall between the end of January and the end of February, Chinese distribute red envelopes stuffed with cash to family members, employees, and others to whom they want to express gratitude. The amount of money inside the envelopes will vary depending on the relationship between the giver and the receiver. Housewives, responsible for managing a family, may distribute dozens of red envelopes with nominal amounts of cash to their grocer, their hairdresser, taxi drivers, and the children of close friends. Meanwhile business executives will be expected to give more substantial amounts to their personal assistants and other people on whom they rely. Children in extended families will receive amounts that in the West would be the equivalent of a Christmas or a birthday present.

Red envelope giving has its roots in Chinese tradition: it happens at a specific time of the year, red is considered good luck for the giver, and the given amount must end in an even digit as this is also viewed as good luck. However, the custom also serves a practical purpose. It is a nonverbal way for the Chinese to acknowledge all those people around them. Outsiders may view the custom as very transactional: a reward in return for favors or services rendered. That would be an accurate perception, as many Chinese relationships with people outside their family circle are unashamedly transactional. Being capable of distributing appropriate amounts of cash during the Chinese New Year and giving them to the right people is obviously an exercise in adding to one's face account.

While established norms and tradition are critical to all Chinese relationships, this is also a society that is going through extraordinary economic change and is being exposed to global trends as never before. Social observers have remarked that these changes have inevitably had an impact on Chinese social mores, particularly among the very young who are more willing to experiment with new social trends.

Yue-Sai Kan, a Chinese-American businesswoman who was named in 2012 as one of the Forbes' list of "Asia's 50 Power Business Women," believes new generations of Chinese engage one another in a more straightforward manner and are far less constrained by traditional Chinese forms of hierarchy and rigid structure. Kan, who is a household name in China through her television shows, books, and her widely successful cosmetics company, has worked in China for the last 30 years and has witnessed firsthand the changes in society. "Young Chinese are very different from their parents. They are much more vocal," she has said, adding that new generations are more uninhibited about acknowledging their friends and peers and this is having an impact on Chinese businesses as well as on families. She believes technology has contributed to this trend and that the electronic chatter transmitted via mobile devices has helped flatten social relationships.

Like many people in China, Kan also worries that the one-child policy, a state-sponsored family planning program introduced 35 years ago that limits Chinese couples in urban settings to having no more than one child, risks creating a generation of socially disadvantaged individuals. These children often receive the undivided attention not just of their parents but of two sets of grandparents as they may be the only grandchildren in a family. With no siblings with whom to learn how to share or to negotiate, the children are described as "little emperors" whose every request is granted. "It is a generation of children who take everything for granted," said Kan. "I sometimes think they don't know how to thank adults for everything that is given to them," she said. This undoubtedly will have consequences in all aspects of life and work.

When working in China, one of the most difficult things foreign companies have to realize, she believes, is that employees have very little loyalty to the company. Chinese workers will get training from one company, and they will not hesitate to jump to another one within a year. Money, not loyalty, is their major concern. Kan herself has absorbed the "tell it like it is, good or bad" American style she was exposed to over the years by living some of the time in New York. "I tell them what I see, and they like it! Some of them became wealthy as a result of working in my company. So they accept what I tell them and they appreciate it—they thank me for it." Kan takes pleasure in both training and acknowledging the hard work and good efforts of young people—for example, the young women who compete in the Miss Universe China Pageants in which she is involved. She is extremely proud of the great progress they make under her supervision in order to compete and place, and Chinese tradition or not, she is happy to let them know about it.

So what advice on acknowledgment should one offer to a visitor traveling to Japan or China for the first time? While visitors must be sensitive to local mores, above all they should be true to themselves.

Both Japanese and Chinese mostly understand that foreigners bring with them a different set of behavioral codes and give them plenty of margin. It would be unnatural for a foreigner to attempt to act like a local, and both Japanese and Chinese would consider it awkward to see one do so. While they may sometimes appear embarrassed by a foreign colleague who shows too much emotion or who is too emphatic in his or her expressions of affection, more often than not, they will endure the courtesy respectfully.

LEADING PEOPLE POSITIVELY AND GETTING GREAT RESULTS IN THE UNITED KINGDOM

Christopher Howell, CPCC, ORSCC, is a management consultant and professional relationship systems coach with around 30 years of successful organizational change experience. Christopher has a background in psychology, business analysis, and project management up to the senior level in many different industries. He specializes in the influencing of alignment through relationships and communication.

> *The deepest craving in human beings is the need to be appreciated.*
> —WILLIAM JAMES, PSYCHOLOGIST

He looked at me with a disconsolate frown. "All they ever do at work is criticize us," he said. I felt the energy in the room dissipate, replaced by a deepening melancholy. Everyone knew what he was talking about.

Criticism appears to be the norm in many organization and team cultures. This does not have to be the case. Successful leaders in the United Kingdom today recognize the importance of giving acknowledgment. Great leaders have always recognized this. Acknowledgment builds positivity in cultures. Research shows that having the right level of positivity in relationships and teams is vital for creating stable relationships and high performance. Giving acknowledgment requires some skill yet is a simple practice and delivers enormous benefit.

In my experience in the United Kingdom, criticism comes from a well-intentioned expectation of high standards. The expectation becomes a belief that high standard delivery is the norm, so anything below standard is an exception. Statements such as "That is what he is paid to do" exemplify the belief in practice. It is then a simple step to assume that feedback is required only when performance is below standard. The feedback is biased toward the negative, and the impact of this criticism is always the same. It depletes energy rather than stimulates it.

Last week, I was shown a letter by a community leader who works in a large volunteer organization. The letter came from his new boss. The letter went through several pages listing everything that he had done wrong over the past six months, and it ended with saying the failings would have to stop. The boss's intention was, no doubt, to raise standards, yet the impact was to demotivate the community leader considerably. You might assume from this that the community leader had been demonstrating low standards. In fact, the opposite was the case. Several of the incidents referred to in the letter were occasions when the community leader and his part of the organization were being honored by the community for their continued high standards of service.

When criticism is applied at the wrong time, or in the wrong way, it has the opposite outcome to that intended. Standards can drop, and resentment can build. When criticism is delivered in a constructive way at the right time, it can also have a positive effect. A culture in which criticism can go either way is in the education sector. While working with different schools, I observed a high level of self-criticism among the more experienced and more ambitious teachers. Self-criticism is valued in education as teachers often work unsupervised with a class. They are expected to monitor their own behavior, and self-reflection is being used much more often as part of the learning process in education so teachers need to model this behavior for the students. Having high expectations of self and others is important, especially when working with children. Research has shown that when teachers have higher expectations of their students, the students achieve better results. Teachers are required to assess student performance constantly, so judgment of others is a necessary practice. This blend of high expectation, high level of judgment, self-criticism, and pressure to perform leads to the high risk of a culture of criticism in the education field. Occasional horror stories emerge of unfulfilled children's lives stunted by inappropriate criticism received at school. Yet the best and most experienced teachers transform the majority of children's lives amazingly for the better.

If a bias toward criticism becomes the norm in the culture of an organization or team, fear levels rise, trust goes down, people take fewer risks so innovation and creativity decline, communication becomes less open, and productivity and performance drop. Ultimately, a culture of criticism can cause an organization to fail. A culture of criticism is therefore an early indicator of system breakdown.

The direct opposite of a culture of criticism is to develop a culture of acknowledgment. Englishman Sir Richard Branson built the amazingly successful global brand of Virgin on a belief about people that he freely expresses. Branson explains:

> Our people do it with style and panache. They have fun. They try to bring good value for money, they try to make sure that the quality is better than any other company around, and they try to do it ethically.
>
> —From http://www.thinkwithgoogle.com/quarterly/people /executive-insight-richard-branson.html, April 24, 2012

It feels so good when something we have done well is recognized and acknowledged. Receiving that recognition delivered authentically and accurately creates a positive energy that can transform subsequent negative experiences. During the deepening economic crisis in 2011, a well-established U.K. events company had some bad news to give a supplier. It was going to be a difficult meeting. The supplier was going to have to take an immediate loss, cutting 100 percent of its substantial termination fees or the events company would not survive. This was worth £10s of thousands to the supplier. The events company executives started the meeting by telling the supplier how good the relationship had been. They admired the facilities and told the supplier how happy they were with the supplier's service. The executives talked about the trust established between them over the years. They were open and transparent about the situation and the potential consequences. By the end of the meeting, the supplier's representatives themselves offered to let the events company go without paying. The two companies parted with excellent goodwill on both sides, and the events company was saved.

Using acknowledgment increases the positive energy and builds trust. U.K. organizations with renowned great leadership commonly emphasize positive valuing of staff to motivate people:

> To ensure the continued success of M&S, . . . it is not just what we do but how we do it but . . . behaving considerately to our colleagues, ensuring that we and they feel valued, motivated, and rewarded.
>
> —From *M&S Annual Report 2011*, April 24, 2012,
> http://annualreport.marksandspencer.com/governance
> /governance-report/leadership.aspx

Successful leaders today know that it is important to create that energy on a team. Ted Corcoran was the first from the Republic of Ireland to achieve the role of international president of Toastmasters in 2003 and 2004, a global organization with over 230,000 members at that time. Ted says on giving recognition:

> Recognize and appreciate them, then recognize and appreciate them some more.
>
> —Ted Corcoran, *The Leadership Bus*, 2008, p. 69

Giving recognition has long been included in basic leadership training for the military. John Adair, developer of "Action-Centered Leadership" and once the leadership training advisor at the Royal Military Academy Sandhurst, England, wrote about motivating others through giving recognition:

It is equally important to encourage a climate where each person recognizes the worth or value of the contribution of other members of the team. For it is recognition by our peers, discerning equals or colleagues, that we value even more than the praise of superiors. We are social animals, and we thirst for the esteem of others. Without fairly regular payments by others into that deposit account, it is hard to maintain the balance of our own self-esteem.

—John Adair, *Understanding Motivation*, 1990, p. 101

The outcome of giving effective acknowledgment is to give people a sense that they are seen, accepted, and valued for their contribution. It therefore increases trust and so allows people to take greater personal risks.

Building a culture of acknowledgment in an organization therefore promotes innovation and creativity, increases positive energy, and facilitates collaboration. These are essential foundations for enabling collective intelligence and for motivating high-performance teams.

Academic research into relationship conflict and into high-performance teams supports the importance of making positive statements. John Gottman (1999) observed conflicts between couples for over 20 years. He found that in relationships that survive and do well, partners give each other feedback in a ratio of 5:1 positive statements to negative, even in the middle of a heated conflict. In relationships that are less likely to survive, the ratio of positive to negative statements reduces and is significantly lower at 0.77. Gottman described this ratio as the best predictor of stability in the couple's relationship.

Marcial Losada and Emily Heaphy (2004) performed research on business teams and found ratios of positive to negative statements similar to the research results found by Gottman with couple relationships:

- High-performing teams had a ratio of 5.6 positive to 1 negative statements in meetings.
- Medium-performing teams had a ratio of 1.9.
- Low-performing teams had a ratio of 0.363 positive to negative statements.

Losada and Heaphy (2004) further observed the following:

High-performance teams were characterized by an atmosphere of buoyancy that lasted during the whole meeting. By showing appreciation and encouragement to other members of the team, they created emotional spaces that were expansive and opened possibilities for action and creativity as shown in their strategic mission statements. In stark contrast, low-performance teams operated in very restrictive emotional spaces created by lack of mutual support and enthusiasm, often in an atmosphere charged with distrust and cynicism.

So giving acknowledgment and showing appreciation for other people create a culture that is much more conducive to positive energy, creativity, and opening up possibilities.

Both the experiential evidence from successful leaders and research results point to the benefit of generating positive energy in human relations. Part of the difficulty with giving acknowledgment is the lack of awareness and skill in doing so. When it is not practiced regularly, like any skill, the capability diminishes. For successful leaders, seeking to give acknowledgment becomes a way of being:

Level 5 leaders look out the window to apportion credit to factors outside themselves when things go well (and if they cannot find a specific person or event to give credit to, they credit good luck). At the same time, they look in the mirror to apportion responsibility, never blaming bad luck when things go poorly.

—Jim Collins, *Good to Great*, p. 35

The skill required for acknowledgment is described well by Laura Whitworth, et al.:

Acknowledgment recognizes the inner character of the person to whom it is addressed. More than what that person did, or what it means to the sender, acknowledgment highlights who the sender sees. . . . Acknowledgment often highlights a value that clients honored in taking the action.

—Whitworth et al., 2007, p. 45

Practicing the skill of acknowledgment demands increasing awareness of other people. Acknowledgment is about what you see positively in other people. It is about who they are being rather than what they are doing: "You had courage in taking that decision." "I see your excellence." "You are committed to what you are doing." "I appreciate your care." "You inspire us." "You are a light that gives us hope."

Excessive negative criticism saps the energy, and a culture of negative criticism is an early indicator of system breakdown. The opposite culture to that of criticism is a culture of acknowledgment. Criticism given with honesty and authenticity and within a context of acknowledgment can be very positive. Critical to the culture outcome is the ratio of positive to negative statements. Research shows the optimum ratio for high-performance teams is just in excess of 5 to 1, positive to negative.

Teams that achieve this ratio are able to maximize their performance, build trust, increase creativity, and open up possibilities for action. Great leaders are very aware of giving positive acknowledgment, show appreciation, and constantly seek to give credit to others. Thus, being skilled at delivering effective acknowledgment is a path to increasing success in personal relationships, raising team performance, and being effective leaders.

Bibliographic References

John Adair, *Understanding Motivation*, 1990.

Dale Carnegie, *How to Win Friends and Influence People*, Cedar reprint. 1990.

Jim Collins, *Good to Great: Why Some Companies Make the Leap and Others Don't*, Random House, 2001.

Ted Corcoran, *The Leadership Bus*, AuthorHouse, United Kingdom, 2008.

Robert Dilts, *Tools for Dreamers: Strategies for Creativity and the Structure of Innovation*, Meta Publications, 1991.

John Gottman and Nan Silver, *The Seven Principles for Making Marriage Work*, Orion Books, 1999.

Marcial Losada and Emily Heaphy, "The Role of Positivity and Connectivity in the Performance of Business Teams," *American Behaviorial Scientist*, vol. 47, no. 6, February 2004, pp. 740–765.

Judith W. Umlas, *The Power of Acknowledgment*, IIL Publishing, New York, 2006.

Laura Whitworth, Karen Kimsey-Howe, Henry Kimsey-House, and Phillip Sandahl, *Co-Active Coaching: New Skills for Coaching People Toward Success in Work and Life*, 2nd ed., Davies-Black Publishing, 2007.

Chapter 15

TRUE STORIES ABOUT ACKNOWLEDGMENT

INTEGRATING THE POWER OF ACKNOWLEDGMENT WITH LEADERSHIP IN A PROJECT MANAGEMENT ENVIRONMENT

Harold Kerzner (PhD, MS engineering, and MBA) is a senior executive director with International Institute for Learning. He is a globally recognized expert in the areas of project, program, and portfolio management and strategic planning. A prolific speaker, Dr. Kerzner is also the author of 45 textbooks, including Project Management: A Systems Approach to Planning, Scheduling and Controlling, *now in its tenth edition, and* Project Management Metrics, KPIs, and Dashboards, a Guide to Measuring and Monitoring Project Performance.

Being a project manager can be a stressful position. Often project managers have a great deal of responsibility with little authority to provide common managerial incentives such as promotions, pay increases, or time off. The project manager may not have any voice in who gets chosen to work on the project and may not be able to remove an unproductive team member. These factors combined with short deadlines and often inadequate resources increase the difficulties of the project manager's work.

The following are several real scenarios common to project management challenges. Please work with your team to think about how you could provide the kind of acknowledgment that you think would be useful and helpful to the individual team members and the team as a whole in the situations described in these scenarios.

Situation 1. An Executive Approach to Acknowledgment

You have just completed a three-day seminar on project management and are somewhat disappointed with the class because the participants did not seem that interested in project management. It appeared that project management was considered as a "second job" rather than their primary job. Experience has taught you that people sometimes are not motivated by add-on jobs unless they can somehow see the benefits. Rewards generally come from one's primary job.

At the end of the seminar, you are invited to have dinner with several of the executives. They want your feedback on how you felt the class had gone. During the discussion over dinner, you ask, "How does the company provide acknowledgment, recognition, and rewards to people that see project management as add-on work, without any career path opportunities as project managers?"

The vice president for engineering responds, "We reward only the project manager, and it is done in secret with a bonus. We do not want to alienate any of the members of the project team." This confirms the attitudes of the people in your class.

What are your recommendations for ways to use acknowledgment and recognition to improve project management interest and performance?

Provide the following to the group as part of the debriefing.

Some possible lessons learned from this situation include the following:

- Project management is a team effort. It is important to acknowledge the efforts of the team members, not just the project manager.

- Rewarding project managers in secret or providing acknowledgment in secret doesn't work. People will eventually find out. The result will be that the people on the team will feel as though they were exploited, and they will not want to work with that project manager again. Project management will suffer severely.

- People might forgive the company for providing a verbal acknowledgment to the project manager without mentioning the project team. But when the company reinforces its actions with monetary rewards, then they will feel cheated and exploited.

Situation 2. The Newspaper Acknowledgment

A company in the Midwest formed a project team composed of 30 people to develop a new product. Most of the people were assigned full time to the project. The project had a very high priority in the company, and everyone knew how important it was. Senior management continuously interfaced with the project team, reminding them of the importance of meeting deadlines and the time-to-market product launch date.

The team performed admirably. The company decided to publicly acknowledge the performance of the project team, and it took out a full-page ad in the local newspaper stating that the new product had been developed and was ready for launch. On the full-page ad were the pictures of just the project manager and the assistant project manager with a paragraph from the corporate executives thanking them for a job well done. Now, the team felt exploited.

What were some ways that the executive team from the company could have used acknowledgment to make this a real win-win situation?

Provide the following to the group as part of the debriefing.

Some of the lessons to be learned from this include the following:

- In almost all cases, the success of a project is the result of a team effort. Acknowledgment of the team would have been the best approach.
- When a team feels exploited, the members of the team will not be happy working for the same project managers again for fear that the same situation will be repeated.

Situation 3. The Union Worker

There are situations in which the success of the project can be attributed to just a few workers or even one worker. This situation occurred several years ago in a company that had a two-year contract to manufacture components for a client. Right from the start, the project was struggling, and the company was afraid that the project would fail. The project team could not deliver the product quality the client requested using the existing manufacturing process.

One of the team members was a blue-collar worker who was a member of the company's union. The worker had an idea for how the manufacturing process could be improved for this client. The company was already behind schedule on this project, and rather than cancel the project and incur penalty costs, the project manager got permission from senior management to allow the worker to experiment with modifications to the manufacturing process.

The worker had to work extensive overtime (paid, of course) and numerous weekends. Everyone in the company knew that if the project were to be successful, it was primarily due to the efforts of one and only one person. The modification worked exceptionally well, and the project was completed just a bit late. The customer was very pleased with the project and the accompanying quality.

The president of the company publicly acknowledged that the project was a success and identified the name of this worker in the acknowledgment. The other members of the team were also acknowledged but not by name. The president felt obligated to reinforce the acknowledgment in some meaningful way for this one worker. Because the worker belonged to a union, the worker had to abide by union policy for promotions or salary increases.

What are some creative ideas about how the president could provide acknowledgment and reward for the one outstanding worker within the constraints of the union contract?

Provide the following to the group as part of the debriefing.

What actually happened and the lessons learned:

The president came up with an idea. The president called the worker into his office, handed him the corporate credit card, and told him to take his family on a company-paid vacation to the Caribbean for a week.

The president knew he was taking a chance doing this and was unsure how the union would respond. After the worker returned from this vacation, the president of the union sent a letter to the president of the company commending him and the company for the way that appreciation and acknowledgment were shown to the worker for what he did for the company. The union members now believed that this could happen to any of them if they demonstrated superior performance.

Some possible lessons learned from this situation include the following:

- Acknowledgment of a single individual rather than the team is acceptable if everyone truly understands the accomplishments made by this individual.
- Providing the worker with a credit card rather than giving him hard cash was acceptable to the union. Had the company given the worker cash, there probably would have been complaints and possibly a union grievance filed.
- Acknowledgment can produce very favorable results if done appropriately.

Situation 4. Executive-Level Acknowledgment

Katie was placed in charge of a two-year project for her company. Her team of 30 employees would be assigned full time for the duration of the project. This was actually a pilot project, designed by the president of the company, to see if project management could work effectively. Most companies test out project management with small pilot projects. However, the president believed that, if project management could work on a project of this size, then it could work on all projects.

At the end of the fourth month, Katie found that several of the workers on her team were threatening to resign from the company if they had to stay in project management. Katie had prepared a detailed project schedule that identified all of the deliverables that had to be provided every Friday for the two-year duration of the project. The people were unhappy with the pressure they were under, and they wanted to go back to the former way of managing—namely, laissez-faire management by which the workers could set their own targets.

What kind of acknowledgment approaches might help to mitigate this growingly negative situation?

Provide the following to the group as part of the debriefing.

What actually happened and the lessons learned:

It was obvious that acknowledgment would be helpful, but who should provide the acknowledgment? Katie explained her problem to the president of the company. The president said that he would attend the next team meeting and talk to the team. At the next team meeting, the president acknowledged the efforts of the team and stated how proud senior management was of their accomplishments. The president also stated that, as long as he was the president, project management would be here to stay in the company and the only excuse for getting off of the project was "death." After that acknowledgment by the president, nobody ever again said anything about getting off the project or leaving the company.

Some possible lessons to be learned from this situation include the following:

- It is important that the right person provide the acknowledgment. In this case, acknowledgment by the president certainly carried more weight than any acknowledgment that Katie could provide.
- The timing of the acknowledgment is important. Katie recognized the importance of acknowledgment early on in the project. Had she waited too long to provide the acknowledgment, people may have left the project team or even resigned from the company.
- The wording of the acknowledgment is critical. By stating that all of senior management was proud of the accomplishments thus far by the team, it made it appear that the acknowledgment came from all of senior management rather than just the president.

SITUATION 5. THE NATURAL DISASTER

Paul was placed in charge of a high-priority project for an external client. The project's completion date of the end of January was considered sacred, and large penalties were associated with late delivery of the products. Paul's project team was staffed by some of the best workers in the company. But even with the best workers, there are always some issues that occur that may be beyond the capabilities of the team members.

By the end of November, the project was two weeks behind schedule, and there was not much hope of catching up. In the first week of December, a disaster occurred when a dam burst and flooded a town. Several members of Paul's team had friends and some relatives that resided in the town. The majority of Paul's team members went to their functional manager, requesting to take a week off from work, using vacation days if necessary, to help fellow church members dig out whatever belongings they could salvage. The functional managers knew of the two-week delay in the schedule, and they told the team members that the final decision would be up to the project manager, Paul.

Paul knew that letting the people go would incur another week's delay in the schedule. Paul told the team members that they had his blessing to go. Paul knew that they would probably go anyway even if he told them to stay. The customer was quite unhappy with this occurrence but understood the reasons. The customer also stated that the penalty clauses would still be in effect because of the delay in the schedule.

The people on Paul's team were actually gone for two weeks rather than one week. The project was now a month behind schedule.

In what ways could acknowledgment be used to save this project?

Provide the following to the group as part of the debriefing.

What actually happened and the lessons learned:

When the team reconvened, Paul provided praise and acknowledgment for the team and for what they did for their fellow church members, and he stated that there are sometimes things in life that are more important than the project. The team was quite surprised to hear this, and they appreciated what Paul had said.

In fact, the team was so appreciative of Paul's acknowledgment and support for their actions that the team came up with a contingency plan: the project team would work, without pay if necessary, the last two weeks in December and part of the first week in January when the plant was normally closed. Most of the team had worked more than 80 hours a week during the last two weeks in December. By the end of the first week in January, the project was back on schedule. The company paid the workers for the time they spent on the project during the scheduled plant shutdown period.

Some possible lessons learned from this situation include the following:

- The power of acknowledgment can produce results better than you can possibly predict.
- The power of a project team to correct a bad situation is remarkable.
- Had Paul not provided acknowledgment for the workers when they returned back to work, and if he had simply stressed how upset the customer was instead, it is unlikely that the team would have come up with this contingency plan.
- The quality of life is often more important to many people than a single project.

Remember, providing acknowledgment in the workplace can have incredible results, big or small. Even a small sign of acknowledgment makes a difference.

ACKNOWLEDGMENT IS ESPECIALLY IMPORTANT FOR CONTINUOUS PROCESS IMPROVEMENT ENDEAVORS

Harry Rever (SSMBP, PMP, MBA, CSSMBB, CSSBB, CQM, CQC, PMP) is the director of Six Sigma for the International Institute for Learning. He has over 23 years of experience in the field of process improvement, Six Sigma, project management, and training. Harry is a dynamic presenter and practitioner of Six Sigma and project management, and he has an innate ability to teach the concepts of quality improvement in an understandable, fun, and more importantly, applicable manner. He currently authors a monthly column, "Ask Harry," on the allPM.com website. Harry is a member of the Project Management Institute (PMI) and a senior member of the American Society for Quality (ASQ).

Most managers and staff personnel are involved in some kind of continuous process improvement effort on a fairly regular basis. Businesses in all industries constantly strive to improve their respective metrics and processes. Projects focus on metrics such as reducing costs, reducing cycle times, improving accuracy rates, and improving productivity, just to name a few. So those project managers and teams that are assigned the never-ending task of continuous improvement need a healthy and regular dose of acknowledgment for their efforts because, as we all know, pushing for improvement requires change, and change comes with resistance. So the power of acknowledgment is vitally important to keep those continuous improvement leaders motivated and appreciated. The following true case studies are examples of the application of acknowledgment for process improvement projects.

Situation 1. Call Center Process Improvement Effort

A process improvement project team was charged with improving productivity in a call center environment. The team was led by the call center's area manager and supported by a Six Sigma Green Belt. The team was composed of managers and union service representatives from the office. This was a particularly challenging project as there was a tremendous amount of pressure from senior leadership for this project to be a success. Measureable improvement was not only needed but was expected. The team was under a lot of pressure, and to make things a bit more stressful, they were somewhat unfamiliar with how to tackle a process improvement project.

With the guidance of the Six Sigma Green Belt, the team defined the problem and then verified the measurement system before collecting data on identified key metrics. The team mapped out the process in detail. They then used various tools and techniques, including cause-and-effect diagrams, Pareto analysis, and regression analysis, to get to the root causes of the problems. After determining the root causes, they brainstormed improvement ideas and tested those ideas in a designed experiment, and they found out, with statistical validity, how to improve productivity metrics. The result was significant, measureable improvement worth several million dollars to the company.

The team leader and the Green Belt did not have any budget authority to reward or recognize the team with bonuses, gifts, or incentives. The team worked very long hours over a six-month period to make the project a success. The project was so successful that it was used as an example to other parts of the business on how to implement process improvement initiatives within the company. What could the team leader and Green Belt do to recognize the hard work of the team?

Provide the following to the group as part of the debriefing.

Discuss the options for acknowledgment.

Feedback: What Actually Happened

- The Green Belt and team leader arranged for the team to give a formal presentation to the company's executive leadership team.
- For many, this was the first time they had ever presented, let alone to top management.
- The business leaders recognized the team and team member contributions.
- The team was acknowledged in a company newsletter with a picture and synopsis of the project.
- For several team members, this project was a significant contributor to their future advancement opportunities.

Situation 2. Leading Change Within an Organization

A vice president of a business unit within a large corporation was trying to change the culture of his organization to one of continuous improvement thinking. He wanted his directors and managers to make better decisions, to use facts and data in the decision-making process, and to do a better job of measuring the impact of improvement efforts. Of course, changing a business culture was not an easy task, especially since the VP was far removed from the day-to-day details of the work being done in the field.

So the VP solicited support from a portion of his staff to lead the change effort. A small group on his staff was charged with engaging the organization on continuous improvement, project management, measuring performance, and basically basing decisions on facts and data. Resistance from the field was immense. Field managers are busy, and they don't particularly like having corporate staff in their business. So they were anything but cooperative and forthright. Thus the staff faced many, many obstacles and were routinely "fed to the lions" by the field.

Nevertheless, the staff assigned to this task, over the course of a year, was relentless and made huge headway in gaining support and setting up a new way of thinking in the organization. The vice president was extremely pleased with the staff's progress although he still wanted more—after all, he's a continuous improvement guy.

How could the VP acknowledge the efforts of his staff without seeming to show favoritism to the field personnel for his staff direct reports? What if the VP did nothing to acknowledge the efforts of this team?

Provide the following to the group as part of the debriefing.

What are the options for acknowledgment?

- Recognize the staff at the annual organization awards banquet in addition to giving awards to the field personnel.
- Write personal thank-you notes to the staff and take them to a nice lunch with the VP and the VP's senior directors (a staff-only acknowledgment lunch with the business leaders).
- Give the individual staff members a year-end "team award bonus" for their special project.

The VP may have a "that is your job" mentality or an "I acknowledge only field personnel, never staff" approach to managing his staff. In that case, what might happen if there are no acknowledgments?

- The staff might eventually feel unappreciated, resulting in loss of motivation and eventual turnover.
- The VP might get a reputation for not being thankful and for being difficult to work for. The result would be an inability to get the best personnel for staff support given the challenging work conditions and stressful environment.

Appendix A: Grateful Leader Definition and Opportunity for Reflection

Definition of *Grateful Leaders*

On an ongoing basis, Grateful Leaders see, recognize, and express appreciation and gratitude for their employees' and other stakeholders' contributions and their passionate engagement. These leaders really want to know their employees, customers, members of the general public, suppliers, and others as people. They give their employees and other stakeholders access to themselves as well as to other leaders regularly. By creating a culture of acknowledgment and appreciation in their organization, in which people truly feel valued, these leaders motivate their followers to strive for continuous improvement and always greater results. This in turn promotes a positive environment and the overall well-being of both the leaders and their followers.

QUESTIONS FOR REFLECTION

Please note that the Grateful Leader Profiles in Chapter 12 were created based on each leader's responses to the questions below, some of which have been adapted for this exercise, along with follow-up interviews. These questions will help you reflect on your current behavior with respect to Grateful Leadership and the approach taken in your organization. If upon completion of your responses to these questions, you consider yourself to be a model of Grateful Leadership, or know someone else who is one, I would love the opportunity to interview you or your recommended person and share the resulting Grateful Leader Profile with our interested audiences (e.g., visitors to www.GratefulLeadership.com).

If some of the questions are too much of a stretch for where you are at this moment, just keep them in mind for future growth and enhancements to your leadership style. Remember that you are already walking on this powerful path, no matter how far along you are, and it's just a matter of degree of manifestation—it is already showing up and is clearly making a difference.

Interview Questions
1. Do you see yourself as a Grateful Leader, and, assuming you do, what does this mean to you? If you do not, what do you feel is missing?
2. Are you a naturally grateful person, or did you have to learn or teach yourself to be grateful to others who work with and for you? What inspired you to practice gratitude in your leadership?
3. Do you think your people see you as a Grateful Leader? What do you base this on?
4. How do these factors fit into your leadership style and strategy?

5. What kind of programmatic evidence is there in your company, inside or outside of your areas of control, that demonstrate your gratitude, or Grateful Leadership style?
   - What recognition, reward, acknowledgment, or appreciation programs or reminders have you instituted or do you carry out—examples of ongoing processes?
   - How do you show appreciation for your people's gifts, talents, and contributions, both formally and informally?
6. Have you taken any steps to formalize your stand—for example, is acknowledgment part of your organization's mission statement, your core values, or are there programs that encourage your managers to embody your philosophy?
7. Have you made any connections between the degree to which your people feel valued and their performance? Have you conducted any surveys that show this connection? If so, would you be willing to share any of these with us?
8. Since sincere and heartfelt acknowledgments can go as far or even farther than plaques and rewards, how do you make sure yours is a true culture of appreciation?
9. What else would you like to say about being a Grateful Leader and how it affects you personally—how it makes you feel as you prepare for your day, go through it, and remember it?
10. What advice do you have for other leaders who are not "there" yet but want to be?
11. Please make sure to include examples/stories of your Grateful Leadership and how that leadership has affected the people you lead.

Appendix B:
Leadership by
Acknowledgment

By Inez O. Ng

As the title indicated, this article is all about acknowledgment. So, why do I want to spend time on this subject? Because if you become better at the art of acknowledgment and use this skill more often, it will change your relationships with others for the better. This skill is especially impactful if you are in a leadership position. It will help you inspire your team, instead of just motivating them.

When you acknowledge someone, you are articulating what it is about this person that you appreciate, admire, like, are inspired by, etc. In recognition, you are showing appreciation for an action. When you acknowledge someone, you are showing appreciation for who they are and how they are behaving. That is the big difference between an acknowledgment and recognition. Many people give recognition well, and very few offer acknowledgment well.

Let me illustrate with an example. Monthly reports are due in five days and the data is vital in the next phase of planning for your department. John, whose job it is to prepare the reports, is unfortunately selected for jury duty and will be out for at least a couple of weeks. Sally, who is in the department and is somewhat familiar with the reports, steps up and takes on the responsibility of completing them on time. The task required her to stay late every day, and to defer work on some of her own projects. So, at the end of the week, the reports are done, but Sally now has to play catch up for her own responsibilities.

If you were to only **recognize** Sally, what you might say is: "Sally, I really appreciated your stepping in and completing the monthly reports. Because of your efforts, we met our deadline and the company can complete the planning as scheduled."

If you were to **acknowledge** Sally, what you might say is, "Sally, I really want to acknowledge your commitment to this department and this company when you stepped in and handled the report preparation. I also want to show my appreciation for your selflessness in placing the needs of the company first, and your dedication when you put in all those extra hours. You are a great team player, and I am so grateful to have you on my team."

Can you spot the difference between the two statements? Recognition places emphasis on the action and results—what the person accomplished. Acknowledgment places emphasis on the person—what qualities they exhibit in order to achieve the accomplishment. It is much more personal and shows a deeper understanding and appreciation of the individual. And it is much harder to do well.

Now back to my example, both statements are nice for Sally to hear, but which one do you think will have a greater impact on her? Which one do you think makes her feel more valued? That is the gift of an acknowledgment. You have to really know something about a person to be able to sincerely acknowledge him/her.

I remember one acknowledgment I received that actually brought up such strong emotions in me that I started to cry. What I was thinking as I heard this person say certain words about me was "how could she possibly see this aspect of me? I can't believe that she knows me this well!" When someone really gets the essence of who you are and they acknowledge you, it lands with a huge impact and it is extremely gratifying.

So, I'd like to suggest that you practice the art of acknowledgment instead of recognition. Be sincere and honest, and notice what impact you have on the recipient. If you are skeptical, try it out on your family first, or try it out on yourself. What would you like to be acknowledged for? Write it down and say it aloud to yourself.

The first skill of an effective leader is to be able to connect with those you are leading. Being skillful in the art of acknowledgment will help you in this aspect of leadership. I encourage you to start practicing today. You will see the impact in the loyalty and dedication your team exhibits just because you noticed and acknowledged who they are.

About the Author: Personal Coach Inez Ng has worked with professionals seeking a smooth and rapid transition from manager to inspiring leader. While focusing on specific areas, her coaching positively impacts all areas of her clients' lives. Contact Inez.Ng@gmail.com

Note: You're welcome to "reprint" this article online as long as it remains complete and unaltered (including the "About the Author" at the end), and you send a copy of your reprint to Inez.Ng@gmail.com.

APPENDIX C: 360-DEGREE LEADERSHIP AND ACKNOWLEDGMENT ANALYSIS

As part of an ongoing Leadership Improvement Program, it can be very valuable to assess employees' competencies in using acknowledgment as a tool for motivation, inspiration, and engagement of the people they lead. You may use this informal 360-Degree Leadership and Acknowledgment Analysis as a starting point.

The assessment will take approximately 15 minutes to complete. It must be completed in one sitting. You may also send this on to your manager, a peer, and a subordinate with the same instructions to complete it.

Thank you for your participation.

1. Strives to create a work environment in which employees are praised for good work.
   a) Never
   b) Occasionally
   c) 50 percent of the time
   d) Most of the time
   e) Always
   f) Not applicable

2. Uses acknowledgment to inspire a corporate culture in which employees have high energy, a great work ethic, and a high level of engagement.
   a) Never
   b) Occasionally
   c) 50 percent of the time
   d) Most of the time
   e) Always
   f) Not applicable

3. Generates a condition of valuing people such that they feel they can have positive and effective interactions.
   a) Never
   b) Occasionally
   c) 50 percent of the time
   d) Most of the time
   e) Always
   f) Not applicable

4. Encourages, motivates, and inspires great work from employees by recognizing and praising the positive contributions they make.
   a) Never
   b) Occasionally
   c) 50 percent of the time
   d) Most of the time
   e) Always
   f) Not applicable

5. Sees the opportunity to deliver a heartfelt, truthful acknowledgment to an employee and delivers it immediately.
   a) Never
   b) Occasionally
   c) 50 percent of the time
   d) Most of the time
   e) Always
   f) Not applicable

6. Sets an example of making acknowledgment the norm, leading to effective changes in behavior that produce ongoing increases in productivity and/or sales.
   a) Never
   b) Occasionally
   c) 50 percent of the time
   d) Most of the time
   e) Always
   f) Not applicable

7. Freely demonstrates authentic and heartfelt acknowledgment when it is deserved, leading to an environment in which people are happier, more loyal to the company, and more motivated to do a great job.
   a) Never
   b) Occasionally
   c) 50 percent of the time
   d) Most of the time
   e) Always
   f) Not applicable

8. Treats colleagues with appreciation and values them for their unique contributions.
   a) Never
   b) Occasionally
   c) 50 percent of the time
   d) Most of the time
   e) Always
   f) Not applicable

9. Praises team members on a project for their accomplishments, attitudes, or persistence.
   a) Never
   b) Occasionally
   c) 50 percent of the time
   d) Most of the time
   e) Always
   f) Not applicable

10. Recognizes and thanks anyone in the organization when it is deserved, including employees such as restroom attendants and mail delivery personnel.
    a) Never
    b) Occasionally
    c) 50 percent of the time
    d) Most of the time
    e) Always
    f) Not applicable

11. Demonstrates either ease and comfort—or willingness to be uncomfortable—when delivering a heartfelt and sincere acknowledgment to others when it is deserved.
    a) Never
    b) Occasionally
    c) 50 percent of the time
    d) Most of the time
    e) Always
    f) Not applicable

12. Requests guidance and input in order to create a culture of appreciation for people, in which they know they are valued.
    a) Never
    b) Occasionally
    c) 50 percent of the time
    d) Most of the time
    e) Always
    f) Not applicable

13. Asks for resources such as training in leadership skills that includes acknowledgment, praise, and recognition.
    a) Never
    b) Occasionally
    c) 50 percent of the time
    d) Most of the time
    e) Always
    f) Not applicable

14. Creates an atmosphere of appreciation in which conflicts are easily resolved and people deal with differences in opinion productively.
    a) Never
    b) Occasionally
    c) 50 percent of the time
    d) Most of the time
    e) Always
    f) Not applicable

15. Is recognized as a leader in using the tools of acknowledgment and appreciation, making people feel valued so that they will engage in behavior that leads to high customer retention and maximized sales.
    a) Never
    b) Occasionally
    c) 50 percent of the time
    d) Most of the time
    e) Always
    f) Not applicable

16. Promotes acknowledgment during team and/or organizational meetings.
    a) Never
    b) Occasionally
    c) 50 percent of the time
    d) Most of the time
    e) Always
    f) Not applicable

17. Engages team members in acknowledgment behaviors to build a more effective and cohesive team.
    a) Never
    b) Occasionally
    c) 50 percent of the time
    d) Most of the time
    e) Always
    f) Not applicable

18. Regularly acknowledges the achievements of even marginal performers in the organization when they go above and beyond what is expected in certain areas.
    a) Never
    b) Occasionally
    c) 50 percent of the time
    d) Most of the time
    e) Always
    f) Not applicable

19. Regularly acknowledges customers, vendors, and contractors with whom he or she interacts.
    a) Never
    b) Occasionally
    c) 50 percent of the time
    d) Most of the time
    e) Always
    f) Not applicable

20. Includes acknowledgment as part of his or her annual performance goals.
    a) Never
    b) Occasionally
    c) 50 percent of the time
    d) Most of the time
    e) Always
    f) Not applicable

21. Regularly acknowledges others at work with whom he or she has occasional contact but who are not part of his or her immediate team (for example, other departments, security guards, maintenance engineers, and concession stand operators).
    a) Never
    b) Occasionally
    c) 50 percent of the time
    d) Most of the time
    e) Always
    f) Not applicable

22. Is skilled at balancing the appropriate use of acknowledgment with holding people accountable for outstanding performance.
    a) Never
    b) Occasionally
    c) 50 percent of the time
    d) Most of the time
    e) Always
    f) Not applicable

23. Acknowledges the effort and iterative improvements in the performance of employees' working to develop their skills in certain areas.
    a) Never
    b) Occasionally
    c) 50 percent of the time
    d) Most of the time
    e) Always
    f) Not applicable

24. Builds an environment in which people feel valued and have trust that this is a safe environment in which they can risk making mistakes.
    a) Never
    b) Occasionally
    c) 50 percent of the time
    d) Most of the time
    e) Always
    f) Not applicable

25. Give examples of instances in which he or she has provided acknowledgment and recognition to an individual or a group and describe the impact of this behavior.

26. In this area of recognition and acknowledgment, describe in detail what you would like this individual to:
Do more of:

_____

_____

_____

Stop or do less of:

_____

_____

_____

Change:

_____

_____

_____

The 7 Principles of Acknowledgment for Those Who Aspire to Grateful Leadership

Principle #1:
Acknowledgment is deserved by many, but received by few.

It will be easier to acknowledge those you lead if you start by practicing your acknowledgment skills on people in your organization you don't know very well, or even know personally at all. Then you will begin making your organization and all of its stakeholders happier, healthier, more productive.

Principle #2:
Acknowledgment builds trust and creates powerful interactions.

Acknowledge the people around you directly and fully, especially those with whom you are in a close working relationship. What is it about your executive assistant, your team leader, your boss, your mentor, your oldest colleague, or your subordinate that you want to acknowledge? Look for ways to say how much you value them, and then be prepared for miracles! Show your profound, heartfelt gratitude and appreciation on a regular basis.

Principle #3:
Acknowledgment can help diffuse jealousy and envy.

Acknowledge those you are jealous of, for the very attributes you envy. Watch your resentment diminish and the relationship grow stronger as you grow to accept valuable input from the person you were envying. As a Grateful Leader, you can set the example and model this behavior for others!

Principle #4:
Acknowledgment energizes people— lack of acknowledgment diminishes them.

Recognize and acknowledge good work wherever you find it. It's not true that people only work hard if they worry whether you value them. Quite the opposite! As a Grateful Leader, your gratitude and appreciation motivate and inspire them to go beyond what they perceive as their limits. They will want to give you their best performance and will do whatever that takes.

Principle #5:
Acknowledgment can make a profound difference in a person's life and work.

We have no way of predicting the profoundly positive impact acknowledgments can have upon a person, a team, a company, or a community. Only by delivering them gratefully, spontaneously, and in a heartfelt way can you know and truly understand the remarkable difference they can make.

Principle #6:
Acknowledgment improves physical and emotional well-being.

There is much scientific evidence that gratitude improves overall well-being, alertness and energy, diminishes stress and negativity, thus boosting the immune system. This causes us to believe that when Grateful Leaders acknowledge others, it has similar effects on them, and greatly improves their well-being and sense of purpose. It also improves your own health and well-being to lead in this way.

Principle #7:
Acknowledgment needs to be practiced in different ways.

Develop an acknowledgment repertoire that will help you reach out to the people you lead in the different ways that will be the most meaningful to each person individually. Your gratitude creates the context in which all of this can occur most powerfully.

Notes

CHAPTER 1

1. Judith W. Umlas, "How NOT to Talk to a Pregnant Businesswoman," *Working Woman* magazine, September 1986, p. 136.
2. Ibid., p. 190.
3. *Network*, directed by Sidney Lumet, Metro-Goldwyn-Mayer and United Artists, Ontario and Toronto, DVD, 1976.
4. Judith W. Umlas, *The Power of Acknowledgment*, IIL Publishing, New York, 2006.

CHAPTER 2

1. Robert Greenleaf, "The Servant as Leader," essay on Servant Leadership, Wikipedia, http://en.wikipedia.org/wiki/Servant_leadership#cite _note-0.
2. Emma Johnson, "How to: Become a Servant Leader," *Success Magazine*, March 3, 2012, p. 1, http://www.success.com/articles/1625-how-to-become-a-servant-leader.
3. Ibid.
4. Kevin Freiberg and Jackie Freiberg, *Nuts!*, Broadway Books, New York, 1996, p. 282, as cited in "Herb Kelleher: Southwest Airlines," *American National Business Hall of Fame*, p. 7, http://www.anbhf.org/pdf/kelleher .pdf.

5. Martin Dewhurst, Matthew Guthridge, and Elizabeth Mohr, "Motivating people: Getting beyond money," *McKinsey Quarterly*, November 2009, p.1, http://www.mckinseyquarterly.com/Motivating_people _Getting_beyond_money_2460.

6. See the complete profile of Walter Robb in the Grateful Leader Profiles in Chapter 12.

7. Raj Sisodia, Jag Sheth, and David B. Wolfe, *Firms of Endearment: How World-Class Companies PROFIT from Passion and Purpose*, Pearson Prentice Hall, Upper Saddle River, NJ, 2007, p. 9.

8. Ibid., p. 11.

9. See the complete profile of Walter Robb in the Grateful Leader Profiles in Chapter 12.

10. "In Praise of Gratitude," *Harvard Mental Health Letter*, Harvard Health Publications, Harvard Medical School, 2011, http://www.health .harvard.edu/newsletters/Harvard_Mental_Health_Letter/2011 /November/in-praise-of-gratitude.

CHAPTER 3

1. Stephen R. Covey, *7 Habits of Highly Effective People*, Fireside, New York, 1990, p. 241.

2. Jennifer Robison, "In Praise of Praising Your Employees," *Gallup Management Journal*, 2012, http://gmj.gallup.com/content/25369 /Praise-Praising-Your-Employees.aspx?ref=more#1.

3. Gallup, Inc., "Employee Engagement: A Leading Indicator of Financial Performance," retrieved from http://www.gallup.com/consulting/52 /employee-engagement.aspx.

4. H. G. Heneman and T. A. Judge, 2006. *Staffing Organizations*, 5th ed., McGraw-Hill Irwin, New York, 2006, as cited in D. Allen, Ph.D., *Retaining Talent: A Guide to Analyzing and Managing Employee Turn-over*, SHRM Foundation's Effective Practice Guidelines Series, SHRM Foundation, 2008.

5. Judith W. Umlas, "The Results of Acknowledging Someone Who Challenges US," blog post, from e-mail by Trudy Patterson, March 28, 2008, www.GratefulLeadership.com.

6. Stephen R. Covey, *Principle-Centered Leadership*, Fireside, New York, 1990, 1991, p. 287.

7. Walter Isaacson, "The Real Leadership Lessons of Steve Jobs," *Harvard Business Review*, April 2012, p. 1, http://hbr.org/2012/04/the-real-leadership-lessons-of-steve-jobs/ar/1.

CHAPTER 5

1. Judith W. Umlas, "Did She Have Any Idea How Much Her Years of Service Were Worth to her Company?" blog post, April 21, 2011, www.GratefulLeadership.com.

2. See the complete profile of Captain Daniel Sosnowik in the Grateful Leader Profiles in Chapter 12.

CHAPTER 6

1. Stephen M. R. Covey, *The Speed of Trust*, Free Press, a Division of Simon & Schuster, New York, 2006.

2. Society for Human Resource Management (SHRM) 1997 Retention Practices Survey, as cited in *The Carrot Principle* by Adrian Gostick and Chester Elton, Free Press, a Division of Simon & Schuster, New York, 2007.

3. Story by Ralph, submitted for www.GratefulLeadership.com blog, September 2010.

4. See full article "Leadership by Acknowledgment" by Inez O. Ng in Appendix B. © 2005 Inez O. Ng.

5. See the complete profile of Janis O'Bryan in the Grateful Leader Profiles in Chapter 12.

CHAPTER 7

1. Anonymous religious leader, personal communication.

CHAPTER 8

1. See the complete profile of Xavier Joly in the Grateful Leader Profiles in Chapter 12.
2. See the complete profile of Kimberly Supersano in the Grateful Leader Profiles in Chapter 12.
3. See the complete profile of Roberto Daniel in the Grateful Leader Profiles in Chapter 12.
4. Diane Brady, "Jack Welch: Management Evangelist," *BusinessWeek Online*, October 25, 2004, http://www.businessweek.com/magazine /content/04_43/b3905032_mz072.htm.
5. Towers Watson, *Turbocharging Employee Engagement: The Power of Recognition from Managers, Part 1*, 2010, originally published by Towers Perrin, http://www.towerswatson.com/assets/pdf/629 /Manager-Recognition_Part1_WP_12-24-09.pdf.
6. Towers Watson, *Turbocharging Employee Engagement: The Power of Recognition from Managers*, Part II, 2010, originally published by Towers Perrin, http://www.towerswatson.com/assets/pdf/642/Manager -Recognition_Part2_WP-NEW.pdf, p. 4.

CHAPTER 9

1. Judith W. Umlas, "Leadership and the Power of Acknowledgment: How to Engage, Motivate and Inspire," presented to PMI Finland Chapter, September 30, 2010.
2. See the complete profile of Michael E. Case in the Grateful Leader Profiles in Chapter 12.
3. Harriet Nezer, personal communication, April 20, 2012.

CHAPTER 10

1. "In Praise of Gratitude," *Harvard Mental Health Letter*, Harvard Health Publications, Harvard Medical School, 2011.
2. Tal Ben-Shahar, *Even Happier: A Gratitude Journal for Daily Joy and Lasting Fulfillment*, 1st ed., McGraw-Hill, New York, 2009. This is an Amazon Review of the book: http://www.amazon.com/Even-Happier-Gratitude-Journal-Fulfillment/dp/0071638032.
3. "In Praise of Gratitude," *Harvard Mental Health Letter*.
4. A. M. Wood, S. Joseph, J. Lloyd, and S. Atkins, "Gratitude Influences Sleep Through the Mechanism of Pre-sleep cognitions," *Journal of Psychosomatic Research*, vol. 66, 2009, pp. 43–48. [PubMed], quoted in Randy A. Sansone, MD, and Lori A. Sansone, MD, "Gratitude and Well Being: The Benefits of Appreciation," *Psychiatry* (Edgmont), vol. 7, no. 11, November 2010, pp. 18–22, http://www.ncbi.nlm.nih.gov/pmc/articles/PMC3010965/.
5. J. Nelson and A. G. Harvey, "An Exploration of Pre-Sleep Cognitive Activity in Insomnia: Imagery and Verbal Thought," *British Journal of Clinical Psychology*, vol. 42, 2003, pp. 271–288, as cited in A. M. Wood, et al., "Gratitude and Well-Being: A Review and Theoretical Integration," *Clinical Psychology Review*, 2010, doi:10.1016/j.cpr.2010.03.005.
6. Robert Emmons and Michael E. McCullough, "Counting Blessings Versus Burdens: An Experimental Investigation of Gratitude and Subjective Well-Being in Daily Life," American Psychological Association, *Journal of Personality and Social Psychology*, vol. 84, no. 2, pp. 377–389, 2003, http://greatergood.berkeley.edu/pdfs/GratitudePDFs/6Emmons-BlessingsBurdens.pdf.
7. Tom Moon, MFT, Making Peace with the Past 2: Cultivating Gratitude, 2007, http://www.tommoon.net/articles/makingpeace2.html.
8. See the complete profile of Chaplain Primitivo Davis in the Grateful Leader Profiles in Chapter 12.

9. Adapted from David McLeod and Nita Clark, *Engaging for Success: Enhancing Performance Through Employee Engagement*, Report to Government, p. 12, http://www.berr.gov.uk/files, accessed February 17, 2010.

10. Jennifer Robison, "In Praise of Praising Your Employees: Frequent Recognition Is a Surefire—and Affordable—Way to Boost Employee Engagement," *Gallup Management Journal*, November 2006, http://gmj.gallup.com/content/25369/praise-praising-your-employees .aspx.

11. F. G. Ashby, A. M. Isen, and A. U. Turken, "A Neuropsychological Theory of Positive Affect and Its Influence on Cognition," *Psychological Bulletin*, vol. 106, no. 3, 1999, pp. 529, 531, 533, 534, as cited in Towers Watson, "Turbocharging Employee Engagement: The Power of Recognition from Managers, Part 2," The Circle of Recognition, 2010, www.cdha.nshealth.ca/.../power-recognition-managers-part-two.pdf.

12. Joel and Michelle Levey, "Understanding the Science of Gratitude," Huffpost Healthy Living Blog, July 1, 2011, http://www.huffingtonpost .com/joel-michelle-levey/understanding-gratitude_b_888208.html, accessed May 7, 2012.

13. Jay Quinlan, "Psychoneuroimmunology," *National Federation of Neuro-Linguistic Psychology*, http://www.nfnlp.com/psychoneuroimmunology _quinlan.htm.

14. Rolland McCraty, et al., "The Effects of Emotions on Short-Term Power Spectrum Analysis of Heart Rate Variability," *American Journal of Cardiology*, vol. 76, no. 14, November 15, 1995, pp. 1089–1093, http://www.heartmathbenelux.com/doc/American_Journal_of _Cardiology.pdf.

CHAPTER 11

1. "The Mission of Southwest Airlines," http://www.southwest.com/html /about-southwest/index.html, accessed May 8, 2012.

2. Steve Piork (Press Contact), "Top-Ranked Travel Brands Southwest, Kayak, Royal Caribbean, and Enterprise Continue to Rule the Industry as Brands of the Year According to the 23rd Annual Harris Poll EquiTrend® Study," Yahoo!®Finance, Harris Interactive, April 10, 2012, http://finance.yahoo.com/news/top-ranked-travel-brands-southwest-123000533.html.
3. See the complete profile of Lynn Batara in the Grateful Leader Profiles in Chapter 12.

CHAPTER 14

1. Rochelle Kopp, "Japanese Managers and Performance Recognition," *Japan Close-up*, December 2011.

Acknowledgments

I acknowledge my family first and foremost for all the love, support, and inspiration they have given and continue to give me. My husband Bob (of 45 years and counting) is beyond compare. He still writes me the love letters twice a week (Mondays and Thursdays) that I wrote about in my first book! My awesome daughter, Stefanie, my great son-in-law, Shaun, and their precious daughter, Lilith, are all my joys! My son, Jared, inspires me continuously with his unique way of looking at the world and his great successes that I find out about almost always by accident.

I thank my grandmother Lena Handler for introducing me to the power of acknowledgment when I was a child, as she continuously told me how special I was. It has stayed with me always. My father, Paul Wagreich, DDS, and my mother, Sylvia H. Wagreich, taught my brother Carl and me that we could and would and should be honored to make a difference in the world. They inspired us to do so by their examples. Carl and his beautiful family give me great joy—my caring sister-in-law Edna, my two nephews, Michael and David, who taught me that kids have great aptitude for learning about the power of acknowledgment and inspired me to write *The Power of Acknowledgment for Kids*; my two older nephews, Eric and Peter, who, no doubt inspired by their father, are also dedicated to making a huge difference in the world. My helpful sister-in-law Marilyn Umlas Wachtel is always trying to find resources relevant to acknowledgment and leadership, and has volunteered to accompany me on any of the worldwide voyages I take as part of my "have mission will travel" journey. And I acknowledge my dear in-laws, Harry and Sylvia Umlas, who have passed on, who would have loved to see all of this happen and to whom I owe a wonderful debt of gratitude for the family I have.

I acknowledge my dear friend Barbara Leach-Kelly, who embodied the power of acknowledgment in her much too short life; my loyal friends Kayli and Jerry Goldman and their two wonderful sons, Scott and David, who are my chosen family; nearly life-long and incredibly wise and treasured friends Drs. Jerry and Carol Goldin; my forever, beloved friend Susan Ellen Spar Adams, Esq.; my soul sister and friend Dr. Chrys Ghiraldini; my friend Lisa Shambro, who contributed so much to my first book by organizing a focus group of readers to give their valuable feedback on it; my high school buddy Ralph Spiegel, who always supports all that I do; my dear friends and loyal supporters Alan and Fredda Chalfin; and my valued friend Leora Gaster, whose husband David Gaster first introduced me to E. LaVerne Johnson because he felt we were "supposed to" meet. And was he ever correct! I thank all of these dear friends for their patience, kindness, caring, continuous love and encouragement, support, and contribution to me and to my passion for making the world a better place—a passion they all share.

Heartfelt thanks to my three incredible mentors, coaches, and supporters in my professional life. First and foremost, there is E. LaVerne Johnson, the founder, president, CEO, and true visionary of International Institute for Learning. From the first moment I breathed a word to her about my idea for a book on the power of acknowledgment, she embraced and supported it totally and generously. I thank her from the bottom of my heart for believing in me, for believing in that book and its power to change the world, and for supporting me totally in making this book on Grateful Leadership the best it can be. Our 20 years together at IIL have been a joy to me, also filled with challenges but all of them ones that have helped me discover and subsequently pursue my passion and my mission. I sincerely believe that I could not have done that without her.

Peter Kohler, my boss and mentor at CBS, believed in me, challenged me, and encouraged me to write professionally at WCBS-TV. Yue-Sai Kan, with whom I worked for many years to bring Asian business practices, cultures, and traditions to U.S. audiences via television, modeled and taught me to never take no for an answer in the pursuit of anything I believe in. That teaching has served me well!

I also want to acknowledge the people who have contributed to this book, either through their writing, their editing, their research, or their valuable feedback: Irene Nicholson made an invaluable connection for me with the military for my work and who researched many of the points I knew in my heart but for which I needed "proof"; Lori Milhaven, VP of marketing, allocated valuable resources to help spread the word about the original book and now has wholeheartedly taken this one on; Melli Pini, Andrea Johnson, Therese Miu, and Vanessa Innes help me on a daily basis to get the word out about the power of acknowledgment and Grateful Leadership; Kaylin Berry contributed nobly to the Grateful Leader Profiles; Nolan Voss and Sid Lama are always there to help make something look beautiful; Ian Walcott has always believed in this work and helped me pilot the first Leadership and the Power of Acknowledgment course in Trinidad; Greg Balestrero opened magical doors that have connected me to great people and has believed wholeheartedly in this work, giving this book a close reading with his excellent and valuable feedback; Lynnda Pollio, chief consciousness officer of *Elevate*, took it upon herself to introduce me to some of the wonderful Grateful Leaders who are profiled in this book; Liliana Bukhshteyn could probably get me an audience with the president or the pope if I needed one; Carl Belack has helped make my sometimes too "warm and fuzzy" courses more solid and more suitable for leaders through the Leadership and the Power of Acknowledgment training, while retaining the heart and soul of the work that I so desperately wanted and needed; Nicolas Gauch, my partner in so many exciting IIL projects, has generously carried the load when I needed to focus on this book; Harriet Nezer, PhD, executive leadership coach, reviewed this manuscript in depth and really helped make it flow; Dr. Al Zeitoun of Booz Allen Hamilton provided me with valuable contacts and information; and Suzanne Foley and Tresia Eaves, PMP, contributed to the outstanding Grateful Leader Profiles.

My appreciation to d.b. Roderick, head of IIL Media, who stands for and exemplifies the power of storytelling as a way of reaching people; to Andrea Johnson for her ongoing love, support, and spirit; and to Michael Borges for his desire from the start to get this work out in the world.

I would like to thank Frank P. Saladis, PMP, for being someone I can always turn to for advice, ideas for exercises for my courses, and breakthrough thinking on acknowledgment and leadership.

I take pleasure in thanking and acknowledging Dr. Harold Kerzner, whose encouragement, support, and inspiration over the years have been priceless gifts! I will never forget his gesture of generosity and assistance when it came to creating his valuable contribution to this book, even when it took him out of his traditional writing realms.

I want to thank and acknowledge every one of the Grateful Leaders whom I have profiled in this book (in alphabetical order): Mark Addicks, Lynn Batara, Michael E. Case, Roberto Daniel, Primitivo Davis, Xavier Joly, Tom LaForge, Janis O'Bryan, Walter Robb, Captain Daniel E. Sosnowik, and Kimberly Supersano. Each one is a superb, continuously growing, conscious, caring, beautiful human being as well as an awesome leader. I thank them for their willingness to share their true greatness with the world through this book. And thanks to Doug Rauch, former president of Trader Joe's and current CEO of Conscious Capitalism®, Inc. for stepping forward to contribute the foreword to this book because he believes in it.

I want to thank and acknowledge the wonderful "stars" of the many true anecdotes I have told about in this book. Every one, whether listed by full name and title (for example, ardent supporter of this work, Dean Pattrick of Nokia) or just referred to by first name (by request), is a true and living example of the results of acknowledgment and Grateful Leadership, or the lack thereof. I thank them all for making this book so readable, as I have been told.

Many thanks to the contributors of the articles on acknowledgment around the world: Adrian Dickson, Harry Rever, Guy Grindborg, and Christopher Howell. They helped bring a richness to this book that I greatly value.

I acknowledge my wonderful rabbis, Craig Scheff and Paula Mack Drill, who have inspired me repeatedly with their vision of all of our potential to create Tikkun Olam, or "repair the world."

As soon as my agent, Claire Gerus, of the Claire Gerus Literary Agency, heard about this project, she took it on with gusto, and she worked with me relentlessly to make the proposal right and marketable, and then to make this book happen. She has always believed in the message with all her heart, and that has meant the world to me.

I also want to acknowledge Associate Publisher Mary Glenn for her faith in me and in this book, and Senior Editing Supervisor Janice Race for her keen eye and helpful suggestions.

In conclusion, I must acknowledge every one of you who has picked up this book and will be putting it to use. If you have read it, I promise and assure you that you are firmly on the path of being a Grateful Leader. And that truly makes the difference!

Index

About the Author

 Judith W. Umlas is senior vice president, author, and trainer at International Institute for Learning (IIL), the global corporate training company at which she has worked for the past 20 years. She is the publisher of IIL Publishing, New York, as well as the publisher of allPM.com, the Internet portal for project managers around the globe. She is the author of the groundbreaking book *The Power of Acknowledgment*, copyright 2006, IIL Publishing, New York. This book has been credited with changing workplaces, communities, families, and individual lives by making use of the transformational 7 Principles of Acknowledgment that she developed. She has an upcoming book on *The Power of Acknowledgment for Kids*.

Judith delivers inspiring, motivational, and transformational keynote addresses on Leadership and the Power of Acknowledgment and Grateful Leadership all over the world. She also leads webinars and teaches full-day virtual and traditional courses to organizations such as Volvo AB, the U.S. Army, Prudential, JMP Engineering, the World Bank, Fannie Mae, IBM, AT&T, and the New York Police Department (NYPD). She has trained tens of thousands of people through her leading-edge, highly interactive, and engaging courses and keynotes—with outstanding and long-lasting results. Grateful Leadership and the Power of Acknowledgment are Judith's passion and her mission!

At IIL Judith was the executive producer of more than 25 global satellite broadcasts with such world-renowned presenters as Dr. Joseph Juran, Dr. Harold Kerzner, Dr. Genichi Taguchi, Dr. Margaret Wheatley, Dr. Eli Goldratt, Joel Barker, and CEOs of many Fortune 500 corporations.

Prior to joining International Institute for Learning, Judith Umlas had a career in the television industry. At CBS, where she spent 12 years, she was producer-writer at flagship CBS-owned station WCBS-TV. She wrote, formulated, and produced editorials for the station's management and won numerous awards for these programs. She also directed month-long station television projects on subjects of public importance. Judith later spearheaded programming and fund-raising efforts at a New York City public television station (WNYC-TV).

She resides in upstate New York, with her husband and son, and near her daughter and her family.

About International Institute for Learning, Inc.

IIL is a global leader in training, consulting, coaching and customized course development, and is proud to be the educational provider of choice for many top global companies. IIL's core competencies include Project, Program and Portfolio Management, Business Analysis, Microsoft® Project and Project Server, Lean Six Sigma, PRINCE2®, ITIL®, Leadership and Interpersonal Skills, Corporate Consciousness and Sustainability.

In addition to its wealth of innovative learning solutions, IIL has also established IIL Media, a full service digital video production company; IIL Publishing, a source for business-centered books that educate and engage; IIL Speakers, a very select group of motivational and keynote speakers whose ideas are inspiring business professionals around the world; and www.allPM.com a project management portal offering volumes of information, tools, articles, tips, blogs, and other project-related necessities for today's project managers.

Please visit our website at www.iil.com or to speak to an IIL Team Member, email: Learning@iil.com or call +1 (212) 755-0777.

IIL Global Companies: www.iil.com/worldwide

Bangalore   Beijing   Budapest   Dubai   Frankfurt   Helsinki   Hong Kong   London   Madrid   Mexico City
New York   Paris   São Paulo Seoul   Singapore   Sydney   Tokyo   Toronto

International Institute for Learning (IIL)
110 E. 59th Street, Floor 31 New York, NY, 10022, USA